Mrs. Riddell

Home, sweet home

Vol. I

Mrs. Riddell
Home, sweet home
Vol. I

ISBN/EAN: 9783337121242

Printed in Europe, USA, Canada, Australia, Japan

Cover: Foto ©ninafisch / pixelio.de

More available books at **www.hansebooks.com**

HOME, SWEET HOME.

A Novel.

BY

MRS. RIDDELL,

AUTHOR OF
"GEORGE GEITH," "TOO MUCH ALONE," "THE EARL'S PROMISE,"
ETC.

IN THREE VOLUMES.
VOL. I.

LONDON:
TINSLEY BROTHERS, 8, CATHERINE STREET, STRAND.
1873.

[All rights of Translation and Reproduction are reserved.]

TO

Mrs. FREDERICK NOLAN,

AS

A SLIGHT TOKEN OF THE AUTHOR'S REGARD AND ESTEEM,

THIS BOOK

Is Affectionately Dedicated.

CONTENTS

OF

THE FIRST VOLUME.

CHAP.		PAGE
I.	THE GREAT HOUSE	1
II.	MY WORLDLY PROSPECTS	21
III.	NEWS FROM THE GREAT HOUSE	40
IV.	QUIET TALK	65
V.	AT FAIRPORT	85
VI.	AT THE OPERA	97
VII.	IN THE TWILIGHT	125
VIII.	MISS CLEEVES	140
IX.	I SING	156
X.	OUR VISITOR	168
XI.	I AM DECEIVED	190
XII.	MISS CLEEVES' OPINIONS	220
XIII.	SHADOWS	242
XIV.	MISS WIFFORDE MANŒUVRES	274

Home, Sweet Home.

CHAPTER I.

THE GREAT HOUSE.

 LARGE, old-fashioned, rambling white house, with red-tiled roof, standing high up on the side of a steep green hill; a background of dark fir-trees crowning that hill, belts of plantation running down to a split oak fence; a long broad strip of common-land, the turf smooth and close as velvet; a narrow sandy country road—made up a landscape on which I gazed day after day, and year after year, from the windows of our cottage, till it became photographed on my brain, a very part and parcel of my memory.

It is not often people begin a story by telling what their eyes beheld; but I am compelled to do so, since that house and those trees, the green hillside, the sward across which lay broad shadows and broader patches of sunshine, always pass before my mind's eye when I sit down in the twilight and think about those early days which are now a portion of the long ago.

My own home plays a very small part in the programme memory recalls when compared with that large white house, and the fir plantations reflected dark and grim against the horizon.

In the summer mornings, whilst the dew was still glittering on the grass, I used to look up at "The Great House"—that was the name of the place—and seeing the blinds drawn close and the shutters unopened, speculate concerning the lives led by human beings who lay so long a-bed. In the spring I longed to search the plantations for violets and wood anemones. When the autumn came, and the "family" departed, as was its wont, to a seaside resort some thirty miles distant, I have trespassed amongst the firs in search of pine-cones, whilst all the time there was a terrible fascination for me in the idea of the large deserted rooms, of the high walled-in gardens where the flowers bloomed and the fruit ripened with never a one to admire or enjoy. Whilst winter's snows fell and winter's rain descended I was wont to marvel in what way the occupants of the Great House employed their time. In brief, whether with hand shading my eyes or nose flattened against the window-panes, through mists of driving rain or a veil of softly falling snow, I contemplated the view, that mansion on the hillside with wings—I did not mention the wings containing windows which resembled eyes—proved to me just what the far Western Land did to Columbus.

Bits of strangely carved wood, fruits of unfamiliar hue, were borne over the waters to him, and he longed to go forth and discover the country whence such wonders came. Waifs from that far-away sphere of society floated on the waves of imagination into my heart, and I too, like Columbus, became unconsciously an explorer.

I have been to the Great House in my time. Yes; and to a few other houses, which it is more than possible might never have been visited by me had those trees and that gaunt mansion failed to rear themselves before my childish sight.

Not higher above our modest cottage stood the Great House than the family who abode in it ranked socially above ourselves. The Wiffordes had been "county people" from the beginning of time, and promised to be county people till the end of it. There never was a period of the world's history when a Wifforde of Lovedale had no existence; and for a man in all Fairshire, in which county Lovedale is situated, to be ignorant of the name only proved that he must be a very new comer indeed, and have spent the previous portion of his life in the remotest wilds of England. As for us, there was a time when it would have seemed to me the height of presumption to mention the Motfields and the Wiffordes in the same breath. We were very insignificant folks indeed—insignificant not merely as compared with " county families," but insignificant also as compared with any one above the condition of a labourer. My grandfather had been only a small yeoman, farming his limited acreage of land as his grandfathers did before him; and when his sons after his death agreed amongst themselves and with their mother that the small possession should be sold, and the proceeds applied to portioning their sisters and buying themselves businesses and practices, it was felt that the children of Reuben Motfield were trying to raise themselves in the world; and the wise men of Lovedale shook their heads, and prognosticated that all sorts of evil must fall on those who were not content to remain in that state of life in which it had pleased God to place them.

Probably the only persons in the neighbourhood who approved of the sale were the Misses Wifforde. Reuben Motfield's freehold, situated as it was in the very centre of land belonging to the Wiffordes, had always been to that family as sore a trouble as the vineyard of Naboth the Jezreelite to Ahab. Over and over again had successive Wiffordes offered a potful of money to successive Motfields in exchange for their land; and the consequence of frequent refusals induced in time as keen a feeling of hatred towards the Motfields as the dwellers in the Great House could be supposed to entertain for the family of a mere yeoman.

But they were gentlemen and gentlewomen, those Wiffordes of Lovedale. No doubt, had they set their minds to it, they might have found some means of acquiring the coveted land by other modes than that of purchase. Many a man has been ruined by modern Ahabs for less reason than the desire to annex his inheritance; and as Wifforde after Wifforde came into possession of the Great House, each with the same desire for that Lovedale vineyard, it has often seemed to me marvellous that not one amongst the number ever was tempted to try whether Might could not be proved synonymous with Right.

They did no such thing, however; and when at length the time came for their wishes to be fulfilled—when Motfield's farm was offered to them by private contract—the two middle-aged spinsters, co-heiresses of Sylvester, the last male Wifforde of Lovedale, behaved generously and kindly, as beseemed those on whom had devolved the honour of an honourable house.

They paid the sum asked—and it was high—without murmur or abatement; nay, they did more. Through their agent they intimated to my grandmother that, understanding she was loth to leave Lovedale, and only consented to do so for the advantage of her children, they were willing, if such an arrangement should prove agreeable to her, to lease her the cottage already mentioned, the garden thereunto appertaining, and a small paddock, free of rent, for the remainder of her natural life.

What the meaning of the last words might be I have not the remotest idea; but Mr. Everitt, the agent, insisted upon that phrase being inserted. Supposing, however, my grandmother had lived, say, to the age of one hundred and twenty years, would she, by reason of that being an unnatural term of life, have been in danger of ejectment? Alas! she did not live even to the allotted period; but suppose she had done so, what then?

My grandmother was not very proud. No doubt it was from her side of the house those practical ideas were evolved which led to the sale of Motfield's farm; and she gratefully accepted the Wiffordes' offer, and removed from her old home such of her belongings as the cottage and outbuildings could well contain.

The kitchen appliances, the parlour furniture, enough to fit up three bedrooms completely, a pony and cart, a few fowls, turkeys, geese, and ducks, her favourite pigeons, her best milch cow; these things did my grandmother gather about her.

An active Phyllis and a stout lad completed the *ménage* until my arrival at the cottage, which occurred exactly one year after Motfield's farm was added to the Wifforde estate.

There had been a trouble in the Motfield family once, and I was the outward and visible sign of that trouble. A daughter of the house had been seen by an artist who came down to sketch Lovedale, and who intended to achieve a reputation out of it.

I presume he did not sketch Lovedale well, for he achieved no reputation, either out of that or anything else; but if his painting did not prosper his suit did; and Emily, the youngest of the Motfields, married him against the wishes and without the consent of her parents.

It was said this marriage killed my grandfather. Be this as it may, he never held up his head after the news came to him. He had loved that youngest girl with an exceeding great love, and had been proud of her beauty (the Motfields as a rule were not handsome). When he was out of spirits, or vexed, or cross, no one could so soon win a smile from him as Emmy, whose laugh he used to say was like silver bells; who had dimples and bright eyes and long brown hair, and a tall supple figure; and—who deceived him.

That was the sting. They were a straightforward, unsophisticated race, those yeoman ancestors of mine—blunt and even rude they might be at times; but no neighbour could say he had ever been misled by one of them.

Honest towards men, honester, if that were possible, towards women, cherishing an ideal of what their wives and their daughters should be—which, strangely enough, their wives and daughters realized —the tidings that Emmy, not more than seventeen, had, while feigning compliance with expressed wishes and repeated commands, met Gerald Trenet secretly, and then as secretly left her home and married him, fell like a thunderbolt upon that quiet household.

Not a bit of solace was it either to my grandfather to consider that his daughter had wedded a man who stood higher in the social scale than herself.

Most unaffectedly the Motfields looked down on all people who did "nothing but write or paint"—on all authors, "play-actors," artists. To their intelligence, such persons were the vagrants of society; and save that they neither stole poultry nor told fortunes, my kinsfolk looked upon the whole class as little different from gipsies.

Indeed, it is probable that they considered the gipsies the more influential, since even moderately sensible folk in Lovedale believed the aged crone and the picturesque young woman could read the future; whilst no one had the smallest faith in the power of the "other Bohemians" (I mean no offence) either to make their own fortunes or to prognosticate the fortunes of others; and since I have been about in the world, I find this Lovedale article of faith by no means so uncommon as the Mormonite, for example.

Veiled under a very flimsy interest and

curiosity, both high and low regard men who live by their brains as earning their bread-and-cheese upon a very intangible, suspicious, and greatly to be reprehended sort of fashion. They are sought after as great criminals might be—they are useful at London parties and oppressive country houses—in small provincial circles they serve to point a moral, and give piquancy to many tales ; socially they live in a sort of No Man's Land, which the great and the lowly alike invade. Sometimes they are reported to be earning and spending large sums of money, the earning and the spending being alike begrudged by outsiders. More frequently they just manage to make both ends meet, and then there is general condemnation, as though hundreds and thousands living by their hands were able to do more.

But the Lovedale people were simple in their social creed as they were simple in their habits of life. They believed in the

Wiffordes, the nobility, their member—who was always a Conservative—their clergyman, their minister, their doctor, and themselves.

Their firm faith in themselves served to rivet their faith in other existing institutions, and to render their dislike keen to strangers, who, so to speak, opening the door of the outer world, permitted chill and unfamiliar blasts to sweep through that happy valley.

Accursed were all strangers. Doubly accursed in the eyes of Lovedale was Gerald Trenet, who carried off the rustic belle of that remote region, and broke her heart in London.

Yes, that was the story. The man who steals a wife from her own home and her own kindred, as he did, is not over likely to make a good husband; and so, as I said, he broke her heart, and barely a couple of years after my birth she died, leaving me —all she had to bequeath—to my grandmother.

"I have called her 'Anne,' after you," she wrote. "May she turn out a better girl than I did!" And thus, with a sort of mark on my forehead, I was sent down to the cottage, where I was taken in and cared for.

My childish memory holds the remembrance of no other home than that.

I have no recollection, mercifully perhaps, of any part of my early life which was not spent in Lovedale; no far-away dreams of close rooms, of a smoky city, of harsh words, of shifts and poverty and unhappiness, anteceding the picture I have striven to sketch for you.

I had a father; but when spirit meets spirit on the eternal shore, I shall only recognise him by a very poor miniature he left of himself.

I had a mother, with sad, sad eyes, and a wealth of rippling hair, whose face is familiar to me through the paintings of a now great academician, to whom, when he was but a struggling artist, she sat, thankful for the bread her beauty enabled her thus honestly to buy. No, there was nothing of sorrow, no shadow of shame, in those quiet happy days of childhood.

When about five years of age I remember that the groom, who each morning went down to Lovedale post-office to fetch the letters for the Great House, stopped at our gate and handed in an epistle with a large black seal.

I was out playing in the garden, and he gave it to me. Doubtless other letters from absent sons and daughters had come to my grandmother before this, which I carried in to her carefully, but that was the first of which I "took notice," as nurses say.

And I took notice of it for reasons following:

First, my grandmother took me on her lap and cried over me. I comprehend now—at that voice from the long-ago past—the wells of memory burst their bounds; next, many letters were written to many people; farther, a dressmaker was sent for, and in a couple of days I caught a reflection of myself in the glass—a child clothed in garments black as the raven's wing.

When on the Sunday following I went to chapel with my grandmother, many women kissed me—amongst others, the minister's wife—and called me a "poor darling."

I was not allowed to have out my toys or nurse my doll, except in a stealthy and surreptitious manner. When I escaped into the garden I was recalled indoors. People—even Phyllis before mentioned, and the boy now grown almost to manhood—looked at me compassionately, and spoke to me more kindly, if that were possible, than usual.

Yes, I was an orphan—not in that very peculiar sense of having one parent still living, which constitutes orphanage in modern phraseology, but in very deed.

I had neither father nor mother, and people pitied me. Why, I could not imagine then. Why, understanding fully what my poor father was, I cannot comprehend now.

What would my lot have been, I wonder, had I been dragged up amongst my father's surroundings—far absent from flowers and fields—never instructed in all the love of honesty and self-respect, of truthfulness and personal responsibility, which had descended like a family legend from one to another of the Motfields.

I can fancy my childhood, girlhood, womanhood, as each might under such auspices have been; and I feel, spite of the commiseration I received—that commiseration which the world always gives to children when even the most disreputable of parents are in God's mercy taken from them young—that the Almighty knew what was best for us both, when He took first my mother from the husband who treated her so unkindly, and secondly, that husband before I was of an age to be useful to him in any way. What a life that would have been! How I tremble even now—knowing what I know of some phases of existence—to consider what such Bohemian association must have proved!

The voyage has not been all smooth, my skiff has not sailed into harbour across untroubled waters; but yet—having just caught sight of those seas over which other vessels have tossed, of those rapids down which many a fair bark has rushed to destruction, of those whirlpools which have ingulfed unwary craft, and those awful rocks on which ship after ship has gone to pieces—I feel the compassion society extended to me because Gerald Trenet died before his feet had even touched the threshold of middle age was utterly thrown away.

Nothing indeed became my father so much in his life as leaving it. He had a long time given for repentance, and he repented. Probably had health been restored to him, both illness and remorse would have become mere memories; but it was not to be.

He died in his thirtieth year, and I and a few very inferior paintings were all that remained on earth to tell that Gerald Trenet ever had a being.

But after all, though I have no memory of him, he was my father; and when I, looking at some of those pictures that now hang on the walls of the room in which I write, think of his uncontrolled youth, of his wild life, which could scarce have held an untroubled memory in it—of his lonely sick bed and his bitter repentance—I trust with a trust almost amounting to faith, that if I am ever permitted to enter through the strait gate, I shall find that God has likewise been very merciful to him a sinner.

CHAPTER II.

MY WORLDLY PROSPECTS.

SOME time before his death my father received a legacy. Speaking correctly, indeed, that legacy was the cause of his death.

A distant relative, of whose very existence he was scarcely aware, dying intestate and without any nearer heir, the whole of her modest patrimony, amounting to something like twelve hundred pounds in money, together with a cottage, a quantity of old-fashioned furniture, a silver tea-service, various articles of ancient china, a dog and cat, and a couple of acres of meadow-land, came unexpectedly into his possession, and almost from the hour it did so his fate was sealed.

To a man who has never had five shillings before him in the world, whose life has been a succession of perpetual shifts, twelve hundred pounds seemed an illimitable sum of money, and naturally he set to work spending it at the rate of somewhere about a couple of thousand a year.

The cottage being a picturesque place, covered with wisteria and climbing roses, situated in the midst of soft English scenery, struck his artistic fancy, and so he kept it, and the furniture, and the plate, and the meadow-land, and the dog and cat, and old servant intact, determining that some day he would take three months' holiday, and paint landscapes which the public should appreciate at last and purchase. He now possessed the only things he had previously needed to insure success—money and leisure—that was the way he put the state of the case to one of his friends—and he intended to make a name and a fortune.

Whether on his deathbed it ever occurred

to him that he had also lacked genius and industry, I cannot tell; certainly while he was strong and well, he believed in himself with a faith which almost seemed deserving of a better return. The self he set up as a god and worshipped failed him utterly. It never did anything worth talking about, and it did a great many things that were best not spoken of.

His was a lost, wasted, unprofitable, sad life, so far as man ever knew. Perhaps there may have been another side to the picture which man never saw; but in a purely worldly point of view, his whole existence was a failure. What he might have done with money and leisure in the way of landscape painting, it is impossible to determine, although it seems to me easy to guess; but as he never made but one slight sketch from the day he came into possession of his small fortune, the chances he gave himself of achieving fame were small indeed.

Not in rambles through the woods, not in catching the effects of sunrise on the distant hills, not in reproducing on canvas the river which came brawling under the grey old bridge and pursued its way between banks where grew alder-trees, and brambles, and ferns, and wild flowers, did he spend the holiday he had vaguely purposed to devote to art.

He spent it in dying. There lay the sweet home landscape before him, but his hand was too feeble even to attempt to reproduce it. Other men might make fame and fortune out of it, but for him the dream was over. He had come away from boon companions, away from the rattle of dice and clicking of billiard balls and shuffling of cards, away from the glaring gaslights and the wicked town, to die; and he did it, and they buried him under the shadow of the ivy-covered church-tower in the stillness of a summer evening.

He expressed no wish to see me before he went; indeed, the first intimation my grandmother had of his illness was contained in that letter to which allusion has already been made as announcing his death.

Probably he felt, as he stated in a long narrative which he directed to be forwarded to Lovedale after his decease, that the sight of me would recall memories too painful for endurance; but it is also likely that he dreaded still more an interview with my grandmother, whose heart he had bereaved.

What remained of his fortune he left to her in trust for me. The cottage was to be let, and the income derived from it paid over half-yearly to " the said Anne Motfield, for the maintenance of my beloved daughter Anne Trenet." The money—three hundred pounds—was to be placed in the Funds, and the interest to accumulate till I reached my twelfth year, when, if my grandmother thought fit, a certain portion might be annually withdrawn, in order to permit of my being properly educated. The silver, securely packed, came down to Lovedale likewise in trust for me; as did the paintings to which I have referred.

Altogether I was regarded by the whole Motfield family as a lucky little child; and from the day when, dressed all in black, I accompanied my grandmother on a visit to one of her sons, who dispensed as an apothecary in the nearest large seaport town, I felt an access of civility, on the part of all my uncles and aunts, for which, at my then tender age, I was totally at a loss to account.

I had not grown any less troublesome, or tiresome, or cross, or sulky than on the occasion of previous visits, but I was very rarely reminded of my shortcomings. Farther, my grandmother was not reproached for "spoiling me" and for "indulging me as she had never done any of her own children."

It was not imputed to me as sin that my hair would fall out of curl and my bonnet get awry, neither did I hear any fault-finding on the subject of my new clothes.

Altogether we had a good time, and I know now that my father's death and legacy caused rather a pleasing excitement in the Motfield family. Hitherto they had looked upon me as a troublesome, and likely to be expensive, interloper—the child, not of a struggling, honest, hardworking man, but of a " ne'er-do-weel," whose propensities to Bohemianism, or to strange ways of life, as they expressed it, I had no doubt inherited; but the three hundred pounds, and the cottage, and the silver, caused them to regard me with a certain amount of respect, though not indeed as quite a desirable addition to the family; and as my grandmother presented her daughters and daughters-in-law with rather expensive mourning, I can perfectly understand the diversion in my favour which was so perceptible that I remarked at the apothecary's tea-table, in the presence of strangers, evidently labouring under the impression that I was saying something original—

"Grandma, isn't Aunt Jane kind?" Whereupon a pleased silence fell upon the guests, while Aunt Jane, who had just offered me, contrary to custom, a piece of cake, looked delighted, inspired by which appreciation I took up my parable and proceeded—

"Last time we were here she wasn't kind; she slapped me, and called me a brat."

After that I have a vivid memory of being carried from the room and slapped again; not, however, by Aunt Jane, but by my grandmother, who had not so light a hand in administering punishment as in making pastry.

All excitement, however, must sooner or later pass away, and the flutter and bustle which ensued after my father's death gradually subsided. Although the minister's wife still spoke kindly to me when we came out of Lovedale chapel (my grandmother was a Dissenter), and the stately housekeeper from the Great House occasionally patted me on the shoulder if we overtook her on her way to church, the memory of my orphan condition was gradually forgotten, and by the time my black frocks were worn out, and replaced by more cheerful garments, the fact of my ever having had a father or a mother seemed obliterated from the recollection of our acquaintances, who rarely called me by my proper name, but talked of me as Anne Motfield, or old Mrs. Motfield's little grandchild.

The years came and the years went—years peaceful and happy. I was allowed to run about by myself—much more than children usually are, I fancy—and I used to sit on the big boulders in the stream that ran down from the Great House estate into the quiet valley below, telling myself fairy tales by the hour together, or singing and crooning old-world ditties while I made wreaths and crowns out of the wild flowers I had gathered in the woods.

Few were the story-books our humble home boasted, but I had read them over and over again. From the cottage where my father died had come, with the silver, some boxes that, besides a few old-fashioned brocade dresses, contained sundry volumes, that I devoured by day and dreamt of by night.

Was ever anything more wonderful and more delightful than the tales those old books contained—tales of wild romance—of enchantments—of supernatural appearances—of wizards—of lovely princesses—of cruel stepmothers—of ladies whose beauty was beyond compare—of knights *sans peur et sans reproche?*

There are no such books nowadays—there are no books (of prose) that appeal to the imagination at all; and perhaps that may be the reason the nineteenth century young people are growing up such an unimaginative and practical race.

What every one writes at the present moment, or at least tries to write, is a reflex of actual life—the life we have to live, whether we like it or not. Authors try to reproduce a faithful transcript of the sayings and doings of this weary work-a-day world, through which walk men and women with sad anxious faces—where virtue does not necessarily mean success—where wickedness is often triumphant over innocence—where the guilty thrive and flourish—where beauty is oftentimes a fatal possession—where genius and courage are beaten ignominiously by money and chicanery—and where the battle is always to the strong, and the race to the swift.

It is the world as it has been since Adam and Eve were cast out of Eden that story-tellers now delight in portraying.

For me, give my fancy that garden, with all manner of exquisite fruit and lovely flowers, to wander through, or even a pre-Adamite literature, which shall resemble in some sort the vague delicious reading I drank-in, feeling it indeed possessed all the sweetness of stolen waters.

My grandmother did not approve of much reading on the part of young or old. For a girl to be sufficiently educated meant, to her understanding, that the said girl could read without having to "try back"—that she could spell in three syllables—that she could do her sampler and her seam—that she could add up a column. If, added to this, she had a sufficiently good ear for music to catch up a tune and sing an old-world ballad, Mrs. Motfield considered her accomplished.

Perhaps it was for this reason she rather deferred to her son Isaac's wife, the Aunt Jane already mentioned, who, besides having a wonderful gift for housekeeping, was wont to sing by special request in the evenings, "Cherry Ripe," "The Young Troubadour," "Annie Laurie," and other ditties of the same class and period, which were much admired, and occasionally drew tears from my grandmother's eyes.

Mrs. Isaac Motfield's minstrelsy never caused me to weep; but no doubt this hardness arose from the amount of original sin I am now aware that lady believed my little soul contained.

It was darkly rumoured that Mrs. Isaac, if business went well, intended her talent to be perpetuated in the persons of her children. When they came to suitable years they were to be taught to play the piano, and I believe some overtures were made for the rickety spinet that had come with the books, the brocades, and the legacy.

As the spinet fortunately, however, happened to be mine, and I was not of an age to be a party to its sale, the negotiation fell through, and the Misses Motfield, at a later period of this story, learnt the mysteries of Cramer's exercises on a five-and-a-half octave instrument, manufactured by

Clementi, I should think at about the time of the First Captivity.

Not that it is for me to cast stones at that ancient piano, since I picked out my notes upon a still more venerable spinet.

It was impossible to keep me from that heirloom. Had there been a key to it, I should have been deprived of my greatest source of amusement on wet days; but providentially the key was lost, so I wandered over the notes—one-half of which were dumb—when Mrs. Motfield was busy or absent, to my heart's content.

One day—one memorable day—there came a person who was in the habit of seeing to the welfare of our kitchen clock; a huge thing in a case, with an absurd moon rising above its dial. There was no lock to it either, and as I was in the habit of stopping it when I did not wish to be sent to bed at abnormally early hours, and of putting it forward when I desired the speedy departure of obnoxious visitors, the clock frequently required Mr. Lambton's services.

Not that Mr. Lambton minded how often he called. He liked the snug kitchen—the little table covered with a snowy cloth — the muffins made by my grandmother's own hands — the sweet fresh butter—the newly-laid eggs—the dainty rasher—the strong cup of tea—which were duly prepared for his delectation.

On the day in question, however, his arrival was unexpected, and as Mary chanced to be scrubbing out the kitchen, I took him into the parlour till such time as the tiles should be all clean and ruddy from the administration of spring water, and a final polishing of red brick.

There, anxious to do the honours, I showed him my father's paintings, which he said were "uncommon fine;" the brocades, that he pronounced to be as "grand as anything worn by the Misses Wifforde theirselves;" the books with plates, his judgment of which disappointed me, as he inclined to the opinion they wanted a "dash of colour," whilst I liked the soft shading of black into grey, as I liked the gloom of the woods in bright summer weather. Finally he espied the spinet, whereof, he informed me, he had heard.

"An ancient article; been made a few years."

"Yes," I said, "it is a great deal older than I am."

"Are you sure of that, miss?" he asked, evidently thinking to make fun of me; but I only replied—

"Yes, I am, and I would give anything to make it talk all over."

"Talk all over," he repeated; "whatever does the little lady mean?"

"Why, listen," I answered, and I ran my childish fingers over the keys; "one half of them don't speak, they have not a word to say."

"Miss," he said, after a moment's silence,

"if a person could put that to rights for you, what would you do for him?"

"Give him all I have in the world," I answered; and straight way I rushed off to my own little room, whence I returned with a halfpenny money-box, the top of which I tore off as I came down the narrow stairs.

"Look," I cried, pouring out the contents; "this is all I have now, but grandmamma gives me half-a-crown on Christmas-days and a shilling at Easter, and I shall have five shillings when I am eight years of age, if I try to be a good child till then; and, oh, make my spinet talk, and I will be good, and you shall have everything I get."

Then Mr. Lambton, though he was a very commonplace sort of individual, looked at me half comically and half reproachfully.

"Child," he said, "I would not take the money of an orphan like you, if you counted it out before me in golden guineas; but I will put the wires to rights for you if you will sing me a song."

"I cannot sing," I answered, blushing scarlet, getting hot to my ears in a very agony of shame. "Grandma says I cannot, and so does Aunt Jane, and they do not like me to try."

"Sing for me," he replied; "Mary says you can lilt like a lark."

"Come down the garden, then," I agreed; and so I let him out of the house, along a walk bordered by thyme and marjoram, amongst which our bees kept busy holiday, across the paddock to a point where commenced a steep descent, planted with fir-trees, at the bottom of which the river Love in its summer idleness crept lazily over the stones.

Then, with my face half averted, I began, "The Banks of Allan Water."

Where I had learned the ballad I cannot tell. I only know that before the first verse was half over I had forgotten everything but my song, and never remember anything else till, that song finished, I stood in a surprised silence once more in the familiar world.

Mr. Lambton never spoke a word, and I turned to look at him.

"Miss Annie," he began, "Mary was quite right; but still I do not think it is a good thing for a baby like you to be able to sing like that."

Whereupon we went back to the house together—across the paddock, up the path where the bees were still busy, and into the kitchen, now wearing its usual air of comfort—both slightly dispirited.

"Never more," I decided, "never for ever should any human being ever hear me try to sing again."

For I felt just as if I had committed some sin.

CHAPTER III.

NEWS FROM THE GREAT HOUSE.

THAT the Motfields ever met in solemn conclave to discuss my demerits is unlikely; but that they arrived at a unanimous opinion on the subject is lamentably true.

They decided as with one voice that I was "stupid" and "odd." Even my grandmother, my dear grandmother who loved me, once in a moment of unguarded confidence expressed her regret that I was not more like other girls; and I felt abashed at my shortcomings.

Subsequent experience has rendered me sceptical as to whether being like other girls would materially have benefited my position. However, she was sorry that I did not resemble the race; and I was sorry none the less perhaps because I could think of no means of remedying the evil.

Unhappily, I was myself; and every attempt I made to resemble other people only made the difference more apparent. Alas, in those days it was very true indeed that I was Annie Trenet, and nobody else. Just a child with strong affections, which rarely, however, made themselves demonstrative; a child unblessed by Nature with good looks or the capability of saying clever things; a child who as the years went on grew painfully shy, whose artificial life was that spent amongst grown-up men and women and little girls and boys, but whose real life was passed in holding silent but entrancing interviews with fairies and princesses, with vague kings and queens, with heroines who were miracles of beauty, and heroes like unto nothing since the creation of the world.

"Yes"—as my Aunt Jane said—"it was a very good thing indeed I had been provided for, since I never could have provided for myself." Doubtless the good lady was right; at all events, no circumstance in my career has ever caused a difference in her opinion.

"Some people," she said to me recently, "are born with silver spoons in their mouth;" and although I could not quite understand her grammar, I comprehended that three hundred pounds, with the cottage afore honourably mentioned, had, in her opinion, provided a very enormous ladle for me.

The difficulty in my life as I grew older was, that I could not talk, probably from an intuitive knowledge that if I did talk, I should not be understood.

Dearly I loved my grandmother; but I was well aware she would have regarded the conversations I held with various imaginary personages as the wildest nonsense—

which no doubt they were; but then it is difficult—for me, at least—to enter into the ins and outs of a life the conversations in which are all sense.

I was not in the least like my aunt's children. They could play *Di tanti palpiti* with all its repeats without a great deal of stumbling before a mixed company, and I could not play anything excepting to myself.

To be sure, I was self-taught. I played the old psalm-tunes I heard at chapel, and picked out the songs wherewith Mary propitiated our solitary cow. Farther, when Tom whistled, most likely for want of thought—since no cross-questioning of mine ever elicited an original idea from that taciturn youth—I appropriated the air for myself; but what did all that prove? Simply that I was odd. It was all very well to play from ear, but if you could not read from book, what should an ear profit?

So said my cousins' music-mistress; so said my aunt.

And besides, I could not play, except just in a mooning sort of fashion to myself; and when I sat down to the Clementi five-and-a-half, I had no idea of setting my dress out to advantage on the rickety stool, as was the habit of Jemima Jane.

I liked best to get into the corner with a book, and strive to close my ears to Jemima's performances. Perhaps that was ascribed to envy; and—well, possibly I did sometimes in those days wish to be more like my cousin and less like myself.

Only, surely that was appreciation and not envy. One thing I can certainly state, however—I do not envy Jemima Jane now.

In the town where Uncle Isaac resided— that seaport to which the Misses Wifforde annually repaired for change of air and scene—there were attractions for me quite independent of my cousins' society. First of all, there was the sea, which I loved then as I love it now. The little room at the top of the house which I shared with a couple of the younger children overlooked the shore; and night after night, when they were fast asleep, I used to get up and gaze with what I comprehend to have been a passionate awe and reverence at the waste of waters, sometimes reflecting back the moonlight, at others lying black and sullen under the midnight sky.

Next, there were plenty of people in the streets, and what seemed, in comparison with my lonely home, crowds innumerable—ladies in gay dresses, gentlemen on prancing horses, soldiers in their uniforms—it was a garrison town—sailors in their round shiny hats and blue guernseys, fishermen in sou'-westers, children, tradespeople, great shops with plate-glass windows, boats, beggars, carriages—altogether a wonderful change and excitement for me, for whom, however,

Fairport held two stronger attractions than any I have yet mentioned—its ancient church and the organ that church contained.

I should not like to be buried in the piece of consecrated ground which lies round and about the old church dedicated to St. Stephen; for the graves are so many and the space so small that the earth is like billows, and has by this time raised itself up to the mullioned frames of the painted glass windows. As a child, that burying ground always gave me an idea of the dead moving about in their last resting-place. It looked to me as though they tossed from side to side. Now being less romantic or imaginative, I object to the place on other grounds; and am glad to remember that in all human probability, when my time comes, I shall be followed by a few who love me and by some others to whom God has enabled me to do a kindness, to a little churchyard in a hamlet I wot of, where the morning sun shines brightly on a great square tomb, which has many names inscribed and many tributes engraved upon it, to the memories of men and women who tried to do their duty in that sphere of life in which Providence had placed them.

Spite of its graveyard, however, I remember St. Stephen's with an abiding affection. Religion never seemed to me the same thing in our whitewashed conventicle at Lovedale as it did within the grey walls of the church at Fairport. No doubt the instruction imparted was equally good; but the sentiments I derived were different. Religion at Lovedale was a duty—not altogether disagreeable perhaps, but still a duty; religion at St. Stephen's was to me, at all events, a romance.

People who have gone to church all their lives long, who have never in their childish days been called upon to eat that strong meat which, amongst even the most liberal of Dissenters, is provided impartially for the sucking babe, the middle-aged man, and the octogenarian tottering to the grave, cannot form the faintest idea how the interior of an old church, and the church-service itself, impresses any young person with imaginative tendencies, who has been weaned on the sterner and more forbidding diet of ordinary nonconformist worship.

Monuments with a story to them instead of our bare walls, only relieved by one bald tablet, white marble edged with black, setting forth the virtues of a certain Joshua Sandells, who had largely contributed towards the erection and support of our barn-like edifice; monuments high as the roofs of the side-aisles; monuments to forgotten grandees; monuments that portrayed kneeling lords and ladies; monuments rich in death's-heads, hour-glasses, scythes, and skulls.

More especially there was one I remember—one which I shall remember to my dying day. It was right above the pew we occupied (my aunt was a Churchwoman, and had, of course, carried Uncle Isaac with her), and the inscription on it ran as follows :—

Sacred to the Memory of Captain Edward Arthorp, Lieutenant James Godfrey, Henry George Rogers and Frederick Sunderland, Midshipmen of the ship Cardigan, which foundered on the Gray Rock, January 1st, 1771.

" The Lord on high is mightier than the noise of many waters."

How often I have read and re-read that inscription, I could not repeat ; how vividly the figures of men praying, with drooping flags and broken spars and the ribs of a shipwrecked vessel in the background come back to me, I might never hope to tell.

As easily might I strive to explain the feeling of utter desolation (as regarded man) with which that monument inspired me ; as easily could I make my readers understand how the waves dashing in upon the sea-shore seem even now to bring it before my mind's eye—how, when I hear the choristers chant—

"They that go down to the sea in ships, that do business in great waters;

"These see the works of the Lord, and His wonders in the deep.

"For He commandeth, and raiseth the stormy wind, which lifteth up the waves thereof.

"They mount up to the heaven, they go down again to the depths; their soul is melted because of trouble."
—I see a wild sea-shore, and the Gray Rock where that tragedy happened, lashed by waves white and cruel; I see those men struggling in a last fight for life; I see them buffeting the billows, clinging to spars, trying to seize the rope which always fell short, striving to keep afloat till succour came, passing through a thousand years of torture to add a few years to existence.

To which succeeds a great calm. I am in an old, old church, dimly lighted. The organ swells, and my heart throbs, and down the aisles there floats, chanted by the choristers, "A thousand years are but as a day in His sight."

To the left that monument; a few hundred yards more to the left the grey, desolate, hungry sea; my own little life opening vaguely before me. That is all; and yet perhaps enough to show my relations were right, and I not quite like other girls of my age and station.

More than once, when I was staying at Fairport, the Misses Wifforde were there likewise, taking in their grand manner change of air too. Each afternoon they were wont to drive up and down the parade, rarely, however, looking at the passers-by, but keeping their eyes fastened on the coachman's back-buttons in a fashion which filled me with a great awe and reverence.

Of course, I admired the manner of our ladies when at home in Lovedale; but it impressed me far more when, in the midst of the world and its excitements, they were still sufficiently mistresses of themselves to consider nothing so worthy of admiration as the family crest. It was not frequently, however, that I had opportunities of contemplating this calm indifference to objects external to the house of Wifforde; for it was always the very height of the Fairport season when they went thither for the benefit of the sea-air; and in the height of the season every man and woman in the town either let his or her house or took in lodgers; and as my uncle was no exception to the general rule, even my small person usually proved at that period an article of furniture too much.

The Misses Wifforde had a house of their own on the cliff—a dull-looking abode with a heavy balcony and a great expanse of hall-door, only relieved by a handle as large as a turnip, and an immense knocker, the design of which was a wreath of oak-leaves and a lion's head.

That dwelling was the quintessence of ponderous and long-established respectability; and I shall never forget the amazement I felt when one day I distinctly heard the notes of "Rory O'More" whistled in its balcony.

I could not believe my ears. I looked up; I could not believe my eyes: there stood a young lady, not more than in her first teens, perhaps less still—a young lady leaning over the balcony, looking far seaward, and whistling—ay, as well as our Tom.

It was very rude, but I could not help stopping to listen.

> "He was bold as the hawk,
> She was soft as the dawn,"

the young lady proceeded, breaking off into song; but apparently whistling was more her forte, and she whistled on, swinging her foot up and down against the ironwork in time to the tune.

Suddenly she caught sight of me, and I was made aware of the fact by this sentence—

"Little girl, if you stand there another second, I will drop a bonbon into your open mouth." And she pelted one at me; whereupon I ran off as fast as I could, and stayed as much indoors as possible for a few days, lest the fact of my boldness coming to Miss Wifforde's ears, she should send a detachment of soldiers to my uncle's house, and have me taken off to prison.

From the dormer window of that attic chamber to which, in the season, Mrs. Isaac Motfield's younger children were consigned, I subsequently beheld the young lady who could whistle driving along the parade with the Misses Wifforde. She was clad in spotless muslin; she had on a black-silk pelerine—pelerines obtained at that time, as they have again, under a different name, within the last three years—and a quiet straw bonnet, trimmed with a cool-looking blue-and-white ribbon. Hats had been previously, and have been since, but they were not in those days; not a bit quiet was Missy, and I could perceive that the calm atmosphere which usually pervaded "the ladies" was disturbed. They could not prevent her turning round and laughing at everything which struck her as ludicrous. Miss Wifforde frequently tapped her with the point of her parasol, while Miss Laura spoke to the offender, as it appeared, more in sorrow than in anger. That any one could venture to laugh in the presence of "our ladies" seemed to me nothing short of miraculous; that any one could laugh twice after being rebuked once was a still greater miracle; and yet I saw that girl do it—I saw her almost scream with laughter as she returned, and it appeared to me she was making merry at Miss Wifforde's expense.

Early next morning I awoke with the sun shining full on my face; and long before any one else had even, I believe, turned in bed, the question was settled to my own satisfaction. The poor young lady must be out of her mind; and oh, what a trouble for the Misses Wifforde!

Somehow, from that time there seemed to me a ladder—a long one, it is true, but still a ladder—set up, by which my thoughts might travel to and peep in at the windows of the Great House, the inmates of which were intimate with sorrow.

In this idea I was entirely mistaken; at least, if the Misses Wifforde had sorrows, they were in no way connected with the young lady of the balcony; but it served the purpose of fostering a vague sort of human sympathy towards "our ladies," who had always seemed to my previous imaginings set as far from me as the east is from the west.

Afterwards I knew more about Miss, and also a young gentleman I had once beheld driving down to Lovedale church in the Wifforde carriage. On one bright April afternoon Miss Hunter, my ladies' lady, asked shelter from us till a shower should be over.

The dependents at the Great House had ever been friendly towards our cottage, but not familiar; and I could perceive that my grandmother regarded the request and the visitor with distinguished consideration.

Hospitality was proffered, and Miss Hunter induced first to taste a glass of cowslip wine, which she honoured with her approval, and subsequently to consent to take off her bonnet—it was an immense black erection—and remain for tea.

Over that meal she unbent considerably; and whilst I, having duly put back my chair, and betaken myself and a book to the window-sill, was supposed to be deaf, as I had certainly been dumb, Miss Hunter informed my grandmother that the Misses Wifforde, after long consideration, were agreed as to the advisability of adopting an heir.

"They want to do justice to all parties," the old lady went on; "and as their only near relations are equally close, they have decided to adopt Master Sylvester for the next heir, and that he shall marry Miss Elizabeth."

It was just like arranging a royal marriage; and my grandmother expressed her surprise no more than she might have done had Miss Hunter announced that one of the blood-royal was about to contract an alliance with the Princess Amelia Sophia Agatha Caroline of Popolinasklinski.

"You know," proceeded Miss Hunter, "they are both of them sort of distant cousins to the family; and the family has always kept up its relationships. Mr. Sylvester is the grandson of a cousin of my ladies' father; and Miss Elizabeth's father was son to that Mr. Cleeves who was at one time so much at the Great House in the late Squire's time. You must surely remember him, Mrs. Motfield—a handsome, spirited gentleman; they said he was the best seat on horseback in the county; but he was killed by a fall while hunting, for all that. I believe he and Miss Wifforde would have married; but the Squire set his face against it; for he wanted her to accept Captain Ralph Wifforde, who afterwards died in India. Dear me! there is hardly a lady or gentleman who used to come to the place living now. To think that of all the Wiffordes there is not one of the name left excepting my ladies! The house, as a rule, is quiet as the grave. My ladies cannot bear either to go out visiting or to receive visitors. I do not know how it will be when Mr. Sylvester comes to live with them; for it is not likely a young gentleman could be content with only their society."

"And when is the marriage to take place?" asked my grandmother, as Miss Hunter at length gave her a chance of edging in a question.

"Oh, bless your heart! not for years. Miss Elizabeth is little more than a child; and Mr. Sylvester is, after a manner of speaking, still just a boy; but I believe it is all as good as settled that Mr. Sylvester is to be the heir, and to take the name of Wifforde, and to marry Miss Elizabeth when she is eighteen."

"What sort of a young lady is Miss Elizabeth—is she handsome?"

"Not in my idea," replied Miss Hunter, who was a tall woman, and held herself very erect, and had a Roman nose and high forehead and light-blue eyes, and hair that, despite her years, refused to turn white; "not in my idea. Indeed, what my ladies can see in her passes my understanding. She is a pert little creature, with more knowledge of the world and its ways already than either of them will ever have in their lives. She turns the place upside down when she is in it. She never was at the Great House but once; and every servant was happy the morning she left. She has not a trace of the Wiffordes about her; but she can wind my ladies round her finger. They say she is wonderfully clever; but I am sure I do not know in what way. She could not hem a handkerchief if it were to save her life; and she told me once she thought a square of Axminster carpet would look just as pretty on the footstools as those beautiful groups of flowers that Miss Wifforde worked with her own hands. She calls my ladies dear old things—yes, to their faces; and she will go into the stables, Mr. Ackworth tells me, and walk round the very hoofs of the horses in a way that frightens even the grooms.

"Mr. Ackworth entreated her one day to be more careful lest she should get a kick from one of the horses; but she only broke out laughing, and said in her scornful way—

"'Do you call those things horses? Ah, you should go into the stables at Dacre Park, and see the beauties my uncle has! Horses! why, these creatures could not kick if they tried! If they ever knew how, they must have forgotten the way, I should think, about a hundred years ago.'"

"I wonder at ladies like the Miss Wiffordes enduring such doings," said my grandmother, indignantly.

"We all wonder they have Miss Elizabeth staying with them," was the reply; "but I do not think the person lives who could prevent her doing precisely what she likes. Mr. Ackworth says he cannot account for the Miss Wiffordes' infatuation except on the ground of witchcraft. She goes about the garden whistling——"

"Yes, I heard her once at Fairport," I eagerly interrupted, letting my book fall in my excitement; and had I been a witch, I could not have produced a greater effect.

It was evident that Miss Hunter at all events had forgotten the fact of my presence, and her startled and angry look frightened me as much as my speech had alarmed her.

"Good gracious!" she said, turning to

my grandmother, "I never thought of the child; and here have I been talking to you as, I am sure, I would not have talked to any other person outside of the Great House. Come here, little girl;" and she planted me before her, fixing me with her light blue eyes. "I hope you have learned your Catechism, and the Ten Commandments, and the Lord's Prayer?"

"Yes, ma'am," I answered.

"Then you know what will become of children who go and repeat things it was never intended their ears should have heard?"

"Yes, ma'am."

"And you will try to be a good child, and forget all your grandmother and I have been talking about?"

Once again I should have answered, "Yes, ma'am," but at this juncture my grandmother came to the rescue.

"You may trust Annie," she said. "I have never known her carry a story in or out of any house." Whereupon, moved by sheer gratitude, I began to cry.

Almost immediately afterwards Miss Hunter, declaring she must go, resumed her bonnet, put on her shawl, lifted the skirt of her thick black silk dress till I could see the topmost tuck in her snowy petticoat, and departed, leaving me under the impression that I had, in some dreadful and mysterious manner, been put upon my trial.

CHAPTER IV.

QUIET TALK.

HOW the news which the facile tongue of my lady's lady had so glibly communicated affected the conversation of us humble folk, only people who lead or have led a monotonous life like ours will be able to understand. In the winter's evenings, when, our early tea over, my grandmother sat knitting stockings, while I toiled along the dreary expanse of a long seam, we talked much about the adopted heir and his wife that was to be.

The whole affair had by this time been positively settled, and everybody in the county knew that at Christmas Mr. Sylvester was coming to take up his residence at the Great House, and that in due course he meant to marry Miss Elizabeth, who in the interim was at her own home, undergoing some educational process, which the Misses Wifforde considered would have the effect of rendering her more fitted for the high calling whereto she was destined.

It is only fair to say that every one (the domestics at the Great House alone excepted) felt, so far as we could tell, satisfied with the arrangement proposed. By the county families it was considered an eminently just and prudent proceeding on the part of the owners of the Wifforde estate.

So long as a nearer relative remained, the rich spinsters had naturally felt that the ancestral property was scarcely theirs thus to dispose of; but now, when death had swept every direct heir and heiress off the face of the earth, when the broad acres promised at their death to become bones of contention amongst far-away kinsmen and kinswomen, it seemed both right and fitting that an heir should be named, and brought up to feel that sense of responsibility which always ought to be a characteristic of those likely to become the owners of large estates or great wealth.

And this youth—this Sylvester—had ever been very dear to the ladies at the Great House. Between his mother and themselves there had, up to the time of her death, existed an almost romantic attachment; and it had never been any secret that the Misses Wifforde paid the expenses of his Eton and college career, and that they always intended to provide handsomely for him when he came to man's estate.

All these particulars, and a great many more, my grandmother detailed as we sat at work with one solitary candle between us, thus whiling away the tedium of the December nights; whilst Mary was whiling away the tedium of her evening with a certain young man from the village, who had been devoted to her for some few years. Years were as nothing in that part of the world, which seems to me now the more singular, since they passed so slowly.

I was older than my actual age, and getting somewhat of a companion to that dear old guardian, who found in me one virtue, that of being an admirable listener.

Not one of the tales of lords and ladies was to me more entrancing than my grandmother's old-world talk about the Wiffordes of Lovedale, their friends and their relatives.

Marvellously exciting were her narratives of how she had seen, over and over again, the hounds in full cry, and the huntsmen at full gallop, passing through Motfield's farm. The days of her youth came back no doubt in all their freshness and beauty as she talked, for there was a breath as if of the early morning air hanging about those reminiscences.

"I can remember well," she said, "the

last Squire bringing home his bride. I was a little girl then, less than you are now; but it seems like yesterday that I saw the arches and the flags, the carriages and the prancing horses, that I heard the men hurrahing, while the Squire took off his hat and drove through them bareheaded, and his wife bowed to right and to left. There were dinners and balls, and the whole place used to be one blaze of light. Ay, there were great doings from that time on till her death; but after that it seemed as if the Squire could not bear the sight of friends or strangers.

"She was a beautiful creature. At Court, where they say every lady is beautiful, she was more so than any. I remember the day she died quite well. I was standing at my father's door, when a groom from the Great House rode past like one mad. His horse was covered with white foam, his spurs were bloody—I could see that as he passed; so I ran down the field to where my father and brother were mowing, and cried out that something dreadful must have happened at the Squire's.

"So there had. In half an hour the man and Dr. Elliott passed our house again, riding side by side together.

"'What is the matter?' my father shouted as they went by. But Alick—that was the groom—never stopped. He just turned in his saddle and said, 'My mistress!'

"Before the doctor got there she was dead, and they buried her and the little baby, who would have been heir had he lived, before the next Sunday came round. The Squire, they said, was like a man distraught; he used to cry over her coffin like a child; and I have seen him myself—ay, fifteen years after—standing beside her grave late at night, when he thought no one was about.

"That Mr. Cleeves was a relative of his

wife; and it was said, although he opposed the idea of Miss Dorothea marrying him on account of his being poor and much in debt, still he would have given his consent in the end; indeed, I heard he had sent, telling Mr. Cleeves he might return; but it was too late. He had married some girl without a halfpenny, and Miss Wifforde stayed single for ever after."

"And why did not Miss Laura marry?" I inquired.

"People said she was too fond of her father and sister ever to leave them; but I always had my notion she liked a cousin who did not care very much about her. But there, child, fold up your work, and we will get to bed. Why, it's nine o'clock already, I declare!"

Thus, night after night, the generations of the Wiffordes, and the deeds they did, and the wives they married, and the horses they rode, and the lands they owned, were rehearsed to me; and when my grandmother was not talking about their former doings, she and I spoke softly of Mr. Sylvester and Miss Elizabeth.

Over and over again I repeated when and how I had seen that young lady, and was applauded for my caution in having kept my own counsel.

"Still, you might have told me, Annie," added my grandmother, after the fashion of one person reproaching another for keeping some dainty titbit all to herself.

And, indeed, in our solitary life not sharing any piece of news did seem a piece of wanton greediness; but then, as I said and truly, I was afraid to share it, lest she should be angry at my having ventured to stop even for a moment under the balcony.

The Wiffordes were as gods to me, and I feared the consequences of letting it be known I had intruded even unwittingly into their holy of holies, and in that sacred place heard the profane sound of whistling.

Christmas came, and with it the new

heir. We saw him drive with the Misses Wifforde to church on the Christmas morning; the family chariot was had out for the occasion, and consequently we obtained from behind our curtains a good view of him. A young gentleman of one or two-and-twenty, with brown hair, a broad white forehead, and a grave thoughtful cast of countenance.

"Like the Wiffordes," said my grandmother. My own memory of the family, however, only containing portraits of Miss Laura and Miss Dorothea, two prim and starched old maids, the likeness so apparent to her failed to strike me.

Yes, he had come. Apartments re-papered, re-painted, re-decorated, re-furnished, were set aside for his exclusive use. It was hinted he had a bias for learning, that books written in strange tongues lined the shelves ranged round his private sitting-room; that the library of the Great House, long unused, was to be rearranged; that his aunts—so, for convenience, the household began to style them—were as proud of his learning as they were fond of himself.

And in truth Sylvester Wifforde had in him the making of a most courteous gentleman.

I shall never forget one Sunday when, meeting us suddenly at a turn of the narrow footpath, he stepped aside into the mud of the high road with as much gallantry as though my grandmother had been young and pretty, and his equal.

She curtseyed and thanked him, apologizing likewise. *He* took off his hat and smiled—such a smile, so sweet, so frank, she could speak of nothing else for a week.

Yes, he had come at last, this Mr. Sylvester, this Wifforde in all but name; a gentleman and a scholar. Could any choice have been better than that the ladies at the Great House had made concerning their heir?

He was an admirable horseman too, and

that was well; for I doubt much, had he lacked the capability and the will to go across country, whether, considering the family traditions, he would have been deemed a fit successor to the Wiffordes of old; but he could ride, not a doubt of that. Often when he has been returning home to dinner, a little late probably, since we had finished our tea, I have seen him riding like a very Nimrod along the sandy road; his reins loosely held in one hand, and his other, the whip in it, resting on his thigh; his feet well in the stirrups, his knees griping the saddle, whilst his black horse Templar, delighted to have "got his head," thundered along to the lodge-gates.

Ah! youth is very beautiful to our imagination, if age be very dear to our hearts; youth is the poem, age the tragedy; youth is romance, age something more real and pathetic than reality! That young man was the embodiment of romance to me, and, looking at him, I pitied the two gaunt ladies who, although they might have been young once—a fact it was, however, impossible for me to believe—could never be so any more.

In those days I often marvelled why the Misses Wifforde did not travel, in order to behold those places of which I had read, and which my soul desired; but I marvel at their snail-like existence no longer. Looked up to as gods in Lovedale, regarded as something like royalty in Fairport, what glimpses of the Holy Land, what foreign seas, what unclouded skies, what gigantic mountains, what historic towns, could have compensated to minds constituted like theirs for the full shock of a revelation that there actually existed inhabited countries where the Wiffordes of Lovedale were unknown, where the worship they received from all of us would have seemed as a heathen bowing down before wooden idols?

Sometimes when my imagination was inspired with a reperusal of those beloved books, in the pages of which citrons and oranges grew wild, that were overshadowed with cork-trees, or perhaps choked up altogether by the luxuriant undergrowth of American forests, I would astonish my grandmother by suddenly asking her whether she supposed either of the Misses Wifforde had ever been in Castile, or if she thought Mr. Sylvester would take a journey to Peru.

"Mercy upon us, child!" the dear old soul would answer, "what should people like them want junketing about in foreign parts? It is only sailors and soldiers, and restless idle vagabonds, that ever go to those outlandish places; and whatever it is that keeps your head running upon them passes my comprehension. I am sure you never hear me talk of anything out of Fairshire."

Which was indeed true; and yet her statement failed to produce the effect she evidently thought it ought to have done, for on one particular occasion I answered—

"But, grannie, when you were down at Fairport, and saw the sea, did you never wish to sail away and away to some island where the palms and the cocoa-nuts grow, and where the woods are full of humming-birds and parrots, and where flowers like those that were at the show can be picked wild?"

Whereupon my relative said frankly that she never had; and proceeded farther to declare, she was heart-vexed to find a grandchild of hers filling her mind with such a parcel of rubbish.

No good, she added, could come of dreaming and drawling instead of minding my seam. Books had done more harm in the world than anybody would ever be able to reckon up. It was reading poetry that caused all my poor mother's trouble. It might be well enough for gentlefolk, who had nothing to do except pass the time;

but for such as us, reading was about one of the worst things a girl could take to.

With infinitely more to the same effect, the peroration being that she was much afraid I should never be of use to myself or anybody else—which I felt at the time to be a most unjust remark, as I really did my best to darn our stockings properly, and to keep the singular collection of ornaments our sitting-room boasted free from dust.

Such feeble acts of propitiation to the household deities utterly failed, however, to satisfy my grandmother.

"You are getting a great girl," she was wont to say—her remark must be understood to refer to age, not stature—"and if you are ever to be fit for anything, you ought to be learning. Why, when I was no bigger than you, I could knit a stocking and turn the heel of it as well as I can do now. I had done a sampler, for which my father got a rosewood frame. I could make a pudding; and, a couple of years after, not a loaf of bread or pat of butter was used in the house that I had not the handling of. I sometimes think, as your Aunt Jane says, that you will be fit for nothing but to sit up to a pianoforte playing—and you cannot do that well. I wish I had burnt yonder old thing when it came into the house, and the books with it. You are not a bit like your cousins. They are content to play their tune and come away; but you would like to be strumming morning, noon, and night; and I believe you would, if there was nobody by to hear you. Bless my heart, if the child is not crying again! A body cannot say a word to you now without your beginning to fret."

And this was true. I had a passion for music, which restraint only made more vehement. Now I am aware that, as I grew older, I must, with my temperament, have been just such a trial to my grandmother as a duckling proves to a hen.

Then I knew she was often as great a trial to me as the hen is to the duckling.

Whenever I tried to get off to my beloved pond, she called me back, and clucked me up under the secure but uncomfortable shelter of her wings.

She did not understand such ways. She was afraid I had taken after my father. She should not let me go back again to Fairport; my uncle spoiled me.

Dear, dear grannie, how you loved me through it all! but yet how many a night you have made me sob myself to sleep!

I was the sole duckling amongst the Motfield hens and chickens. What marvel, therefore, that my proclivities should occasion surprise, not to say alarm?

Wishing for what is vain, I often, musing in the twilight, wish with an unutterable longing that the woman who cared for me with such untiring love could have lived to see me now, to understand that it is possible for a duckling to follow its instincts and yet still return safe to land after all.

Perhaps in a better world she has learned what she certainly never thoroughly understood in Lovedale — namely, that even amongst the grandchildren of a yeoman there may be as much difference in temperament, character, and aspirations as amongst those of an earl.

But *any* difference in the members of a family astonished my grandmother. That such a person as Miss Elizabeth Cleeves could have developed—I use the word because " retrograded" might not be strictly correct—out of the Wiffordes, was to her a never-ending source of wonder.

To her, for a creature such as Miss Hunter described to be the product of a respectable series of ancestors, was as great a phenomenon as though our staid cow Cowslip had presented the household with a six-legged calf.

Such things were, it is true; but they

had never been amongst the Motfields till that artist unhappily took it into his head to visit Lovedale. Such things were; but they had never happened amongst the Wiffordes till Mr. Cleeves, thwarted in his design of marrying his cousin, espoused Gertrude, niece of General Dacres, who had been born and passed a considerable part of her life in India, and was generally supposed to have done nothing in her existence except lie on a sofa and read novels.

In my humble way I fear I caused at the cottage as much trouble as Miss Elizabeth to the ladies at the Great House.

Once I saw her ride past with Mr. Sylvester. Yes, she was a hoyden; galloping over the strip of green turf as hard as her horse could go, and all the while turning round in her saddle and laughing at Mr. Sylvester, because he seemed to disapprove of her mad pace.

"Grannie," I asked, "did the Misses Wifforde ride much when they were young?"

"No, child," she answered; "they were always ladies."

From which remark I inferred that, amongst the traditions of the Wifforde family, equestrian exercise for ladies was considered masculine and unbecoming.

CHAPTER V.

AT FAIRPORT.

AMONGST the attractions of Fairport was its theatre, which has not been hitherto mentioned, because until I attained my twelfth year I had not the remotest idea what the inside of a theatre might be like. Externally the building was uninviting. It was a cross between the Methodist chapel and the town-hall, but dirtier than either; and in the season it had bills stuck upon it, as in like manner there were notices of meetings, tolls, rates, and sermons posted on the doors of the other edifices above mentioned.

To me the word "theatre" conveyed no

impression. I could not understand what was meant by acting. That world still remained a *terra incognita;* not even the piece of carved wood referred to in my first chapter had been wafted from the footlights to the shores I inhabited.

The Motfields were not a family given to dissipation. They were a money-saving, home-loving people, and whilst my uncle attended to his customers, my aunt saw to her household. They were ambitious in their way, but it was a modest way. He wanted a plate-glass front for his shop instead of the small panes, which suggested rather than revealed the beauties of his crimson and blue bottles. Her soul longed for a satin dress and a gold chain of a very heavy and cumbersome pattern which obtained at that period of the world's history. Farther, she desired one son should be a curate, the other remaining with his father and the drugs; whilst my uncle's cherished desire was that Jemima Jane, his first-born, should mate with the son of a woollendraper in a large way of business, and who hoped some day to be mayor.

To a certain class in London the title of Lady Mayoress seems a thing to be coveted; and to my uncle it appeared desirable that one of his daughters should be married to the son of a possible provincial mayor.

The origin of such desires being matter past finding out, I can only record his wishes; and deduct therefrom the moral, that a person whose horizon happened to be bounded by them was not in the least degree likely to be in the habit of wasting his shillings and half-crowns on the pit or dress circle of a local theatre.

Once, I believe, he had gone with an order to witness the tragedy of *Damon and Pythias*. Having myself in later times been a spectator of that enlivening play, I can well understand a man might be content ever after to leave the drama as enacted in Fairport to the patronage of his idler and richer neighbours.

But at length there came to Fairport a company the names composing which caused a flutter and excitement amongst all ranks and classes in the town.

Hitherto we had esteemed the young ladies arrayed in scarlet riding-habits and the foreign-looking gentlemen attired in black velvet, who went in procession along the parade on those rare occasions when a large tent was pitched on a certain piece of common land lying outside the town, as amongst the most remarkable of created beings; but now, when rumour declared that the then queen of song was coming, had come, to Fairport, every other feeling gave place to an uncontrollable curiosity to know something about her.

The local papers had each an article on the opera in general and that special opera-singer in particular. Over their cards staid tradesmen dealt out musical and financial gossip; how they understood she had a finer voice than Madame This, That, and The Other, whom more than one said they had heard at Her Majesty's when they visited London in such a year.

A large lithograph of her as Norma appeared in the shop-windows, and it was generally rumoured that the income she derived from her shakes and cadenzas was about equal to that of the county member. In addition to which, we all somehow learnt that her extravagance and her charity were about equally matched, and kept rapid pace together.

She had arrived. It was on a Saturday night that one of the waiters from the Crown Hotel brought the news of her actual appearance to my uncle. They had all arrived, in fact, and the hotel was turned upside down.

Nothing in it pleased any one. The *prima donna* had brought down her own cook, maid, and lap-dog; the tenor was at the moment of his, the waiter's, departure engaged in a stormy interview with the landlord; one of the minor stars had despatched him, the speaker, for eau-de-Cologne, a toothbrush, a box of quill pens, and two sticks of black sealing-wax, with a hurry which scarcely left the man's speech intelligible.

Already every flower in the Fairport nursery-grounds had been cut to decorate the dinner-table; while the chief, or rather chieftainess, of the party had ordered in enough shrubs in pots to convert her apartments into a bower.

Farther, they jabbered together in a language, or rather in many languages, unintelligible to the waiter; they laughed much, they ate much, and they drank more. In fine, he concluded they were a "queer lot;" but "then, all them play-actors were the same;" at least, so he understood. "He had not seen much of them himself, he was glad to say;" such remark being intended as a side-wind at The George, where the tragedians and comedians who occasionally honoured Fairport with their presence were wont to put up.

All these statements my uncle repeated over the supper-table to his wife, and we children, being permitted to sit up on Saturday as well as Sunday evenings to partake of the various dainties provided, had the satisfaction of having our curiosity whetted as our appetites were appeased.

What a night that proved to me! For hours I lay dreaming dreams, wide awake, about that strange land whence these strangers had come ; and when I fell asleep, it was but to wander on into still more unfamiliar scenes, peopled by ladies who wore crowns and gentlemen who strode along with swords by their sides, and who each and all bore some distant family likeness to the circus troupe, as well as to the heroes and heroines whose ideal portraits graced the pages of my favourite volumes.

How eagerly, when morning broke, I longed for the time to arrive when, prayer-books in hand, we should accompany our elders to church, where I had promised myself a sight of the new arrivals!

That any human beings, except beggars, sailors, and maids-of-all-work, should absent themselves from St. Stephen's, was an idea which had never entered into my mind.

Even the very soldiers duly marched up to the sacred edifice, and after service marched away again to the sound of as many musical instruments as are mentioned in the third chapter of the prophet Daniel. Why, then, should the lady, whose features were familiar to me through the medium of the lithograph already mentioned, remain away?

But she did—they all did. They came not to morning service, or to afternoon, or to evening; and my disappointment, though unconfessed, was so great that I could eat nothing, and had in consequence a dose of physic compounded by my uncle's own hands.

It was not easy to swallow, but it was better to take it than confess my folly. So I crept up to bed, and looked out on the sea bathed in the moonlight; and then fell asleep, wondering what it could seem like to be a rich lady, able to go about where and when she chose, and even take a drive instead of going to church.

That, it was darkly whispered, the stranger had done, and what gave colour to the story, was the known fact that several of her party had gone out for a row across the bay.

It was frightfully wicked, but the very wickedness had a fascination for my imagination, stimulated as I now know it to have been by a sermon preached that morning, the gist of which was a commination against all persons who performed plays, all persons who went to witness plays performed, and all persons who wished to witness them.

In church, conscious of my own guilt as regarded the last clause, my soul had, if I may say so, metaphorically hidden herself away beneath the sandals of my shoes. When I came out into the sunshine, however, my spirits revived; and as we walked home along the parade, the moral of the sermon seemed to me much less true than I am bound to say it does now.

Dear to me—ah, how dear no words could ever describe — is the aspect of a well-filled, well-lighted theatre. The very smell of the place recalls memories that can never be quite forgotten till I have ceased remembering; the sound of the instruments makes me feel like a war-horse scenting the battle. Yes, I love play-acting; but I am not quite sure whether the curate of St. Stephen's was not right after all. At all events, there is a wide difference between the doors of Drury-lane, for instance, and the strait and narrow gate.

Clearly my aunt was of that opinion, for she made many disparaging remarks concerning singing men and singing women, about people who could earn as much money in a night as many a hardworking father of a family could in a year. She had a good deal to say also about wickedness in high places, and instituted a considerable number of comparisons between virtue and non-virtue, which then conveyed no meaning to me. Nevertheless, I was glad to get away from the supper-room and the talk, such as it was, to my chamber, looking out over the moonlit sea.

Next evening, spite of the sermon, all the rank and fashion of Fairport flocked to the theatre. I saw plenty of youth and beauty driving past—ladies with ringleted hair, carrying choice bouquets; some coquetting with fans, some leaning a little forward to look out of their carriage-windows. It was a vision of "fair women;" but no human being has ever faithfully described the effect such a vision produces on a woman except the author of *Jane Eyre*, and no one need attempt to do so after her.

Late that night, hours and hours subsequently—so it seemed to me, though the length of time was an entire delusion—I crept from my couch to see those carriages flash back again; and then, after the last had passed and the sound of its horses' hoofs died away down the parade, I crept with a vague mental hunger upon me, back to the little cot, with its white hangings and snowy coverlet, that never after that visit held me again.

CHAPTER VI.

AT THE OPERA.

ON the Thursday following that evening when, to the delight of a crowded audience, *Der Freyschütz* was put upon the boards as creditably as could be expected, considering the limited resources at the manager's command, my Aunt Jane, her eldest son, and her eldest and youngest daughters started off to pay a visit to Daniel Motfield, another uncle of mine, who had established himself in a town some fifteen miles off as a corn-merchant.

He was only a corn-merchant in a very small way; but his wife brought him some money, and as it was known that at her father's death all he possessed would come to her and her children, Mrs. Daniel seemed to my Aunt Jane a person whose friendship was to be desired: a sentiment Mrs. Daniel reciprocated, wherefore the two ladies visited each other as frequently as the intervening fifteen miles of country would permit.

When Mrs. Daniel came to Fairport, she brought some of her children, and remained for a day or two; when Mrs. Isaac Motfield went to Deepley she was invariably accompanied by some of her offspring, who were wont to speak rapturously of the pleasures to be found, and the dainties to be enjoyed, at their Uncle Daniel's house.

Towards myself Mrs. Daniel Motfield adopted a very simple course. Virtually she ignored my existence, of which I have now every reason to believe she at that period strongly disapproved. After kissing my cousins all round, she would indeed so far unbend as to give me one finger that I had to shake, and say—

"Well, Annie, how are you?" or, "So you are here again, Annie?"

Once I remember she gave me six walnuts; but that was because I had, most reluctantly, presented to her a beautiful little needle-book, that had come with the pictures and the brocades and the spinet from the old house where my father died.

Mrs. Daniel still preserves that needle-book, and exhibits it to her acquaintances as a proof of the generous disposition her dear niece possessed even when quite a tiny child—the praise being totally undeserved, as I never gave anything away with less good will in my life.

I did not like Mrs. Daniel; and yet when I stood on the doorstep and saw my cousins drive off in the bright sunshine, my heart was so lonely and sad, that I had much ado to keep from bursting into tears there and then.

So few people cared for me. I tried

hard to be good; but in my case certainly goodness was its own reward, for no one appeared in the smallest degree interested about the matter.

For the moment I almost hated the sight of my cousins' bold healthy faces, as they turned round and waved their hands in farewell.

One of them had insisted on my lending her a brooch, which it was certain she would never return, as she publicly stated to her mother that Annie had given it to her; and I lacked moral courage to enter a protest against the assertion. My grandmother would, I knew, be vexed at its disappearance. She had not wanted me to take it to Fairport, from which place I generally returned home as bare of valuables as a plucked fowl is of feathers; but my entreaties carried the day, and now the brooch was gone, together with a reticule, knitted of blue-silk cord, lined with white silk, and adorned with tassels—another of the small possessions which, my cousin's soul desiring, it had.

And yet I was ungrateful for thinking about these things or feeling hurt because they did not take me with them. Was not a visit to Fairport as much of an "outing" for Annie Trenet as a visit to Deepley for them? Had not my aunt kissed me, and said I was to be sure and take good care of my uncle and Tommy?—the rest of the family being from home. Had she not given directions for a pudding to be made, and a cake baked? Yes, that was all quite true; but I wanted, nevertheless, to have been driving along the road I knew so well from description: through the woods, across the ford, down the long hill to Deepley. I wanted to see Mrs. Daniel's drawing-room, where the blinds were always down, lest the sun should fade the carpet; where the chairs were tied up in brown holland pinafores, that if undone, revealed glimpses of amber damask; where there was a real glass above the chimney-piece, and three painted urns with gilt handles and knobs—my cousins said gold handles and knobs, but I have since rejected this account as fallacious—on the mantelshelf; where there were cabinets filled with foreign shells and feather-fans—the gifts of a brother in the merchant-service; where there was bead-work that faintly shadowed forth Mrs. Daniel's love of the elegances and refinements of life; and where the very table-covers were wrought in tent and cross-stitch, to the admiration of all permitted to behold.

Farther, I desired to ride round the paddock on Dapple, a certain staid pony, who had, I feel confident, a poor life of it when those boisterous young folks took him in hand; and I wished to pick up walnuts myself, and to eat of the fruit of the luscious mulberry-tree, which grew—I knew the very spot—in the middle of a grass-plat, which was, to quote Jemima, "covered and covered with berries, that were always falling from the boughs."

Then there were pet rabbits and an Angola cat, and a little white dog, and a large black one; and not one of these possessions had I ever beheld, although my cousins must have seen them over and over again.

It may not seem much, after all, to have fretted about; but small trials are great to little people, and with a very sorrowful heart I ascended the staircase, and went into the drawing-room, and looked out over the sea. Then I went up another flight, into my aunt's bedroom, and looked over the sea again; after which I took a third view of the same scene from my own chamber.

By this time I felt better, and remembering Tommy, who had been induced to bear the parting from his mother without making public lamentation only by the promise of lozenges, which he was then enjoying, decided on taking that young gentleman out for a walk.

As a rule, Tommy was not a desirable companion; but on this occasion he proved, as his mother would have said, as " good as gold." Whether it was the effect of the lozenges eaten, or of the prospective pudding to be eaten, it is difficult to say; but the usually fractious imp demeaned himself towards me with an amiability and a decorum foreign to his nature.

Did I wish to go on the sands, he did not immediately desire to remain on the parade; did I suggest walking through the town, he was not instantly seized with a passion for collecting shells and sea-weed; and accordingly Tommy and I, with a rare harmony, wandered first along the beach, and returned home by a circuitous route, which led past the terrace and the hotel, and then through that street where the theatre was situated.

There I stopped, and read slowly the

huge flaunting bill, which set forth that on Thursday evening would be performed *Il Barbiere,* and on Saturday *Eurydice*—announcements which dispelled the small amount of cheerfulness acquired during our walk.

Should I ever grow up and go to theatres? Should I ever hear any music different from that in St. Stephen's—anything which should fulfil my ideal of minstrelsy? Should I ever be in the same house with those beautifully dressed ladies I had watched on Monday night, and should be looking at again that evening, as they drove along the parade?

Well might Tommy accuse me of crossness, and threaten to lift up his voice unless I told him a story on the spot; well might my uncle, bringing a healthy appetite with him to dinner, ask me if I were ill, that I sat so silent, and ate nothing.

"I am quite well, thank you, uncle," I answered; but I could not help unbidden tears filling my eyes as I did so, and no doubt he half guessed the source from whence they sprang, for he said, cheerfully and kindly—

"Never mind, my little maid. If Mrs. Daniel does not want you now, somebody else will want you hereafter. Put a bright face on it; there will be money bid for you yet."

Then I did what I dare say astonished him mightily: I got up, and threw my arms round his neck, and put my lips to his, Tommy the while, in an access of amazement, surveying the tableau with his mouth filled so full of pudding, that he had subsequently to swallow it with a gulp.

In that moment I think my uncle's memory leaped back over the barrier of years. He was a boy again, and my mother but a mite of a child, and he and she were wandering through the fields together, bird-nesting, primrose-seeking, butterfly-catching, blackberry-gathering, nutting, as they were wont; for she had been his favourite of all the flock, which was the cause, perhaps, of the comparative kindness I received at the hands of his household.

He was young again, for the moment, and she was alive; but ah, well-a-day! youth passes away like a shadow! And here were he and I—he middle-aged, I a child as she used to be—speaking heart to heart with a sort of mute appeal.

"I tell you what, Nannie," he remarked, after a second's pause: "you and I will walk up to the theatre to-night, and see all the gentlefolk going in to hear the great singer. Should you like that?"

"Oh, uncle!" I exclaimed.

"Me too," put in Tommy; which observation we both ignored, feeling our happiness would not be increased by Tommy's presence; and silence, in his opinion, giving consent, the young gentleman remained satisfied.

What an afternoon that was! What a

glory there seemed over the sea! what a beauty in the sunshine, in the long stretch of sandy beach, in the white-winged vessels, ay, even in the boats drawn up on the shingle! How I devoted myself to Tommy! What tales I told him, what pictures I exhibited before his expressionless eyes, what pains I took with the child, physically and mentally, nobody would believe. We played at cat's-cradle; I taught him the royal game of goose. I seemed lifted up into a sort of seventh heaven, since at length one person seemed vaguely to understand I lacked something necessary to happiness.

For the first time in my life I believe I was that day popular; and I had my reward, yea, in very truth.

Duly set out was the tea-table—thin bread-and-butter and thick slices of bread duly graced the board. Jam appeared in a small glass dish, and the cake, which already Tommy had devoured in anticipation. There likewise was the sugar-basin into which his fingers strayed to such an extent that, finally presenting him with a spoonful, I placed it on the mantelshelf beyond his reach.

Everything was ready excepting the tea. But where was my uncle? How did it happen that he, usually punctual, should not have appeared ere now?

The servant, from whom I sought information, reported him as absent; and Tommy, struggling at the moment to lug a heavy chair to the fireplace in order to reach the sugar-basin, paused in his efforts on hearing her reply, and entreated me to cut the cake.

"It must be cut some time," urged that terrible child, "and pa wont mind."

"If I did anything of the sort, your papa would be excessively angry," I replied, with that calm dignity which befitted my age.

Whereupon Tommy pulled a face at me, and recommenced his infantile labours.

He had just got the chair into position,

and was going to mount it, whilst I, on my part, was about to remove the sugar-basin to a still greater altitude, when my uncle burst into the room.

"Nannie," he cried, "how should you like to go to the opera?"

"Oh, uncle!" I gasped out, like one who had been asked a question too strange to be true.

"I am not jesting, my little girl," he said. "As I was coming down the parade, I met Mr. Bilbay, of the *Flying Mail,* and he said he had a box for four, and that if I would like to hear Madame Serlini, he had two places to spare. So I told him my little niece was music mad, and that if I might bring her too, I would be there. You must put on your best bib and tucker, child, for it is the stage-box, although I do not suppose anybody will notice us."

It was all fairyland after that. In no earthly habitation, I am sure, was the tea poured out that night. In Arcadia I ate a slice of bread-and-butter, and cut Tommy enough cake to make a dyspeptic of him for life. But the digestion of some children is wonderful, and I believe he went to bed more willingly in consequence.

I waited to pour out a third cup of tea for my uncle, who, perceiving the impatience I tried in vain to hide, then said—

"We have not much time to lose, dear. Run upstairs, and put on your best frock, and let us be going. If you have not got a dress of your own good enough for the occasion, look in your cousins' drawers, and take what you need."

But I had a dress with me—a lovely dress, that must, so Miss Hunter declared, have been embroidered in a French convent, and served probably as a christening-robe to some one who lived and died before I was thought of.

My grandmother, thinking it a pity so rare a thing should lie hidden any longer, had brought it forth from amongst the brocades, and made an upper skirt of it for me, which I wore on such rare occasions as a visit to the minister's wife, or a tea-drinking at the schools, over a fine white muslin slip.

The bodice had, under Miss Hunter's advice, been likewise skilfully manipulated; and when I appeared in this attire, with a curious Indian necklace round my throat, and my short hair—it was the custom then for children to wear short hair—brushed out and made to appear as well as possible, Uncle Isaac—arrayed, to my astonishment, in a white tie and a swallow-tailed coat, which latter had done service at his wedding—looked at me approvingly, and said—

"You will do, child. Put on a thick cloak, Nannie," he added, "for you will find it chilly coming out of that warm theatre."

And in two minutes more we were really, actually, truly, on our way to the opera.

I could not believe it possible, and yet still I did believe it. I would have danced along the parade, had not a sense of decorum restrained that ebullition of feeling. The only way in which I permitted my rapture to evidence itself was by giving my uncle's hand, which I held, a great squeeze from time to time.

He too seemed very happy. On the whole, we were just like a couple of children out together for a holiday, too enjoyable to be talked about or fully realized at the time.

When we got into the High Street, he turned into a draper's shop, where the following dialogue took place—

"Good evening, Mr. Nelson."

"Good evening, sir."

"I want a pair of gloves for my little niece. We are going to the opera."

And so the gloves—the first pair of kid I ever had in my life—were bought and paid for, and put on and buttoned by kindly Mrs. Nelson, who stooped down and kissed me when she had effected that feat.

In a drawer upstairs lie two gloves, that, small though they are, were then too large for me; and I never can look at them without a sorrowful longing that I could go back and live that evening over again, and touch once more the hand of him who was thenceforward so stanch and tender in his love.

What a blessed visit that of Mrs. Isaac Motfield to Mrs. Daniel Motfield proved to me! And yet I had been discontented and ready to cry when the party started. I felt ashamed of myself, and in an access of gratitude and happiness gave Uncle Isaac's hand such a terrible squeeze, that he said, laughingly—

"There is no necessity for you to break my bones, Nannie, although we are going to the opera."

"But I can't believe that we are going," was my reply.

"Well, seeing is believing, surely, for here we are," he answered; and, still holding his hand, we threaded our way amongst the carriages that were already blocking up the narrow street, and entered the building.

Of course, having lived so long in Fairport, he was well known to all the people connected with the theatre; and though some of them looked rather astonished at seeing him there, dressed so elaborately, every person was very kind; and whilst one took charge of his hat and overcoat and umbrella, another relieved me of my cloak and bonnet, and a third led us along a narrow passage covered with red carpet, at the extreme end of which he unlocked a little door, and let us into a place close to the stage, hung all round with chintz, and furnished with four chairs, that had red velvet cushions and white enamelled backs.

If fairyland was ever presented to

a child's eyes, fairyland opened before me at that moment. The light, the glitter, the beautifully dressed ladies, the band, the scenery, appeared before me like some unreality produced by the wand of an enchanter.

Was I awake or dreaming? Vainly my eyes looked round the house for an answer, I was stricken dumb and stupid with the sight, and stood like one bewildered, till my uncle, pulling me gently towards him, bade me sit down on one of the back chairs.

"For Mr. and Mrs. Bilbay will be here shortly," he added. "What do you think of it all, Nannie?"

I could not answer. I could only stare at the place in which I found myself with a sort of transfixed wonder.

Experience, which teaches us so much we should be glad never to have learnt, has informed me since, that the Fairport theatre was dirty, shabby, small, and inconvenient; but to my imagination that night it seemed like the palace of a king, or rather like one of those enchanted halls I had read of in Eastern stories— where thousands of lamps shine brightly, where gold and precious stones are strewed about as freely as pebbles on the seashore, where ladies are dressed in the height of magnificence, and the aspect of everything is different from that of our work-a-day world.

Suddenly my eyes perceived in a box on the opposite side some faces which were familiar to me. There, attired in rustling silks, with splendid shawls wrapped round them, with lace and ribbon softening, not concealing, their grey hair, sat the two Misses Wifforde; and there too was Miss Cleeves, restless and unblushing as ever, whilst behind stood Mr. Sylvester, and some other gentleman with him.

Here was a nice state of things! If Miss Wifforde knew we had presumed to come into such high and mighty company, might she not have something done to us?

The terror of caste was very strong upon me as I whispered—

"Do you know, uncle, the ladies from the Great House are here?"

"Well, dear, they will not eat you up, I suppose," he said, more in answer to my terrified expression than to my words; but I doubt if even this fact would have put me at my ease, had not Mrs. Bilbay appeared at the moment—an immense woman, who, good-naturedly insisting on my sitting in the front beside her, fairly enveloped me in the folds of her voluminous skirt.

Mrs. Bilbay was a Londoner who cared as little for the traditions of local greatness as Miss Cleeves herself, and looked round the house through her opera-glass with a coolness which shocked while it inspired me with some degree of confidence.

As for Mr. Bilbay, in comparison to his

wife he appeared much about the same size as a shrimp might beside a large crayfish. Nevertheless it was rumoured he had the stronger will of the two, and successfully managed to get his own way, which was not a bad way either.

"Do you think you shall enjoy it, little one?" she asked, after she had completed her survey of the house and exchanged remarks with her husband about some few of the audience.

"Yes, ma'am," I replied, softly.

My heart was in my mouth with delight, and yet I could find no better answer.

"Monday's performance would have been the one for you to see," she went on; "plenty of movement and spectacle. The music to-night will be lovely, but the plot is very quiet."

Without in the least understanding what she meant, I answered that it would be beautiful to me, which seemed satisfactory to Mrs. Bilbay; for she smiled, and was proceeding to give me an outline of the opera, when her husband said, "Hush!" and the first act commenced.

It had all been unreal enough before, but from that moment I was like one in a dream; and as the opera proceeded, the fascination grew upon me till I forgot the spectators, my companions, and my own identity, in listening to such singing as it seemed to me could be like unto nothing except that of the angels in heaven.

Since those days I have heard almost every noted singer of the time. Many more famous than my particular star have trilled their lays and rehearsed their woes, but to me there can never be such another *prima donna* as Lucia Serlini.

Others might have more magnificent voices, others greater dramatic power, others more perfect and regular beauty; but no one woman ever combined such expression, such grace, such refinement, as she who was the love of my youth.

I did not comprehend, of course, a word she sang. Mrs. Bilbay had placed a book of the opera before me, but it lay on the front of the box unheeded till my uncle removed it for his own private instruction; while I sat and listened spell-bound, quiet, yet with a vague yearning, an unsatisfied longing, in my heart, the cause of which I cannot clearly define even to this hour.

All at once there came a burst of applause louder and more persistent than any which had preceded it. *The* song of the opera was ended, but I naturally was then ignorant of the fact.

"Marvellous!" exclaimed Mr. Bilbay, clapping his hands with all his might.

"Simply perfection!" said his wife.

"What did you think of that, Nannie?" asked my uncle, leaning forward.

And still the storm of applause continued; still the rain of bouquets fell at her feet; still she curtseyed her acknowledgments, moving slowly backward all the time.

Then a tempest of noise arose. A hurricane of encores and bravos swept through the house. The audience clapped and stamped till I thought the place must come down.

"What does it all mean? What do they want?" I whispered to Mrs. Bilbay.

"They want her to sing it again; and see, she is going to do so."

For a moment a greater tumult of applause than ever, more curtseying, more bouquets; next instant a silence which might have been felt, and then, breaking the stillness, came that divine voice singing the first notes of "Home, Sweet Home."

I never heard anything like that woman's rendering of the melody—never in all my life. Already I was worked up to such a pitch of excitement that I could scarcely keep from crying; and when, after the slow " Home — home — sweet — sweet — home," she broke forth, with a sort of passionate assertion, into the next line, " There's no place like home," ending with something which seemed an expression of melancholy regret for home lost for ever— " There's no—place—like home," the tears I had hitherto restrained fell hot and fast on the cushions.

Just then she chanced to look towards our box—through a mist I could see her beautiful eyes resting on me for a second. It was only a momentary glance, but it recalled me to a consciousness of where I chanced to be; and with a swift sense of shame, I wiped my eyes, and clasped my hands tightly together with a determination of not being foolish again.

And I did not shed another tear, and neither Mr. nor Mrs. Bilbay, nor yet my uncle, suspected what I had done until the opera was just finished, when the boxkeeper presented Mr. Bilbay with a twisted-up note written in pencil.

That gentleman read it twice over, and then, handing it to my uncle, remarked—

"The little lady is highly honoured."

After which he passed it on to his wife, who, after perusal, gave the scrap of paper to me, saying at the same time—

"What in the world does that mean, child?"

I read it, and in a moment rose up, dizzy and with my cheeks all aflame.

"Please do not be angry, uncle," I entreated; "but I could not help crying, and the lady saw me—I know she did."

Whereupon Mr. Bilbay and Uncle Isaac exchanged smiles, while the former, patting my shoulder, said—

"I daresay Madame Serlini is not offended with you past forgiveness. Summon up all your courage, and come with me. It will never do to keep her ladyship waiting."

CHAPTER VII.

IN THE TWILIGHT.

THAT night, as we walked home along the parade, and looked out over the moonlit sea, I do not think, in the length and breadth of Great Britain, to say nothing of Ireland and the Channel Islands, there could have been found so happy a little girl as myself.

The beautiful lady, so far from appearing angry, had asked, in her charming imperfect English, with a sweet foreign accent, if I loved music much, who I was, whence I came, if I had brother and sister, mother and father; and when I told her I had neither brothers, sisters, mother, nor father, she gathered me to her heart in silence.

Then, after a moment's pause, she asked

if I should like to come again to the opera on Saturday.

"Uncle Isaac would not be able to bring me, ma'am," I answered.

"Your charming wife will take charge of the child—is it not so, dear sir?" said the lady.

Whereupon Mr. Bilbay promised faithfully that his charming wife would do so; and we came away after Madame Serlini had touched my cheek with her lips, and said—

"Adieu, dear child; we shall meet again."

All of which was duly recounted to my companion as we retraced our steps homeward.

"It was better than going to Mrs. Daniel's, was it not, Nannie?" said my uncle.

"A thousand times over," I answered.

And then we were very unromantic, and

sat down to supper, and discussed the whole opera from beginning to end.

"I do not know much about music myself," said Uncle Isaac; "but I should say that woman's singing is worth all the money we hear she gets for it. Besides, one bad cold might spoil her voice for life; and of course she must put by for a rainy day."

Put by! I listened to this idea with all deference then; but the time arrived when I understood the ludicrous absurdity of bracketing two such incongruous ideas as "saving" and the beautiful *prima donna*.

"You must get to bed now, Nannie," was my uncle's remark, when he mixed himself a glass of punch, and filled the pipe he invariably smoked before retiring to rest. "You must get to bed, or else your aunt will find you with pale cheeks on her return, and scold us both."

Prophetic words, although the scolding

we received was not the result of any delicacy in my appearance.

For the first time almost in my remembrance of the household, there was a serious and angry dispute between husband and wife. My aunt, from some unexplained cause, did not return home in the sweetest of tempers. Something had evidently disturbed her equanimity and touched her vanity—never a difficult feat to perform; and when she heard that her husband had, as she straightforwardly worded her sentence, "been such a fool as to take a child who was uppish enough, and silly enough, and useless enough before, to hear an opera, and get her head stuffed full of ridiculous notions," she emptied the vials of her wrath on our devoted heads.

As for me, I was a "sly, underminded, hypocritical little brat, who would never come to any good, any more than my father had done before me——"

"Remember the child's father is dead,"

broke in my uncle, in a tone I had never heard him use previously.

"The more reason she should be grateful to those who have been mother and father both to her," rejoined my aunt. "No, Isaac; if you are an idiot and bewitched by your niece, I am no idiot, and she cannot delude me. I will have no such sneaking ways in my house. Stuck up in a box at the opera, indeed, like any lady, and kissed by play-actors afterwards! How do you suppose this will fit her for the sort of life you know she must lead? You would not catch any of your own children crying like babies, and putting themselves forward out of doors. No; she is getting too old to be gadding about visiting; and so I shall tell her grandmother. And you thought you would be allowed to go again to-morrow night, did you, miss? By that time you shall be safe at home in Lovedale. I will have no such goings-on in this house so long as I am mistress of it."

"There, Nannie, you have been scolded long enough," broke in my uncle at this juncture. "Run away, and put your things together, and you shall go back by the coach this afternoon. Your aunt is right: there shall be no apple of discord in any house I am master of."

His eyes were very bright, and his colour very high, and his tone almost mocking as he spoke; and I obeyed his commands, understanding intuitively that he had ranged himself on my side, and that there was going to be a dreadful quarrel.

And a dreadful quarrel they had—so Jemima, who listened outside the door, informed me, while I sat sick and faint on the side of my bed, hurt as I had never been hurt before, wounded beyond possibility of cure—thus it seemed to me then—pained to an agony which could not even find expression in tears.

I had been so happy, and I was so wretched. From a seventh heaven of bliss I had been cast down into depths which my soul had never previously fathomed. Most innocently I had caused discord between my uncle and aunt. His very kindness to me was now occasioning him trouble. And still the war went on, till I heard the drawing-room door close with a bang, and my uncle descend the stairs with a haste foreign to his nature.

"Shall I help you to pack up your things?" said Jemima, who, perhaps remembering the brooch, was anxious that my exit should take place before, with mind at ease, I was in a position to expose the fraud practised by her.

"Please," was all I could say; but I could not help watching her while she packed, and noticing that anything of value was left in the drawers, a perquisite for the girl who elected to be my assistant.

From a social position higher than her own I write these lines, and therefore I am quite sure that when she proffered her assistance Jemima's character was that of an embryo lady's-maid, minus the qualities which render a lady's-maid a desirable inmate of a family.

After a time, regardless of trifles, I abandoned my former attitude, and leaving Jemima to appropriate as much as she liked, crept down to my uncle.

"I am going home with you, dear," he said. "I want to see my mother." And accordingly we went home to Lovedale together.

Since that time I have ascertained the ticket intended to admit me and a friend was appropriated by my aunt, who, with Jemima, went to the opera and beheld *Eurydice*.

Eurydice! With my present knowledge of that opera there is to me a wonderful satire in the idea of Mrs. Isaac going to see it at all — she to whom anything but the most unromantic of lower middle-class *convenances* were as Eleusinian mysteries.

Eurydice, with its passion, and its pathos, and its power! what meaning on earth should it convey to a woman whose sole aim in existence it was ultimately to possess a better-furnished drawing-room than Mrs. Daniel, and to see her sons and daughters mated to the daughters and sons of prosperous tradesmen?

All right and proper without question, and above everything, human, but nevertheless so totally prosaic an existence, that it repelled my imagination utterly when I attempted to enter its precincts.

They would have none of me, and for the future I could have none of them; wherefore I returned to Lovedale, to my old life and my old pursuits, bringing back with me to each and all a vague unrest remarkable in one so young.

My sudden return occasioned much grief to the dear grandmother; and but for Uncle Isaac's kindness in accompanying me home, and explaining the circumstances under which I had, so to speak, been expelled in disgrace, I scarcely know how I should have satisfied her of my total innocence of evil in the matter. As it was, she rebuked her son for taking me to such an improper place as a theatre; she said she thought Jane was quite right in insisting on my immediate departure.

"You know well," she went on, "that the child is unlike other children, and has strange-enough ways and notions, without having any more put into her head."

"With all due deference to you, mother," was the reply, "I do not believe you will change Nannie's ways and notions unless you can have her re-created. As Mr. Bilbay said to me last night, she has the true artist nature; and although I fear that nature may not add to her happiness hereafter, still I am certain it would be wise to recognise its existence and treat her accordingly. For some inscrutable reason the Almighty does not make everybody alike, and it seems to me very like waste of time to attempt to change His designs. Here is Nannie, brought up entirely by you, as different from any one of your children, her mother not excepted, as a bluebell is from a thistle. She is a dear good little girl, grateful for very small kindnesses, whom I had not thought much about, or in the slightest degree understood, till yesterday. But I think I do understand her now; at any rate I know that whilst I live she shall never want a friend."

I could not bear it any longer; I crept quietly out of the room where mother and son sat together in the twilight, and went into the garden, and down to the end of the paddock, where I could hear the murmur of the Love as it flowed over the stones far below. There after a time my uncle joined me.

"Nannie," he began, "I did not know you had come back into the room when I was talking to your grandmother, or I should not have spoken as I did. As you did hear what I said, however, I want you to do something for me."

"What is it?" I asked eagerly,—"what is it? I will do anything on earth for you."

"I want you to prove me a true prophet. I want you to be a good girl, who shall comfort your grandmother for all the sorrow your poor mother caused her. I will tell you the story of your mother's marriage, Nannie, and you must never forget the misery it caused."

There, in the twilight, with the moon struggling to climb up high enough to look over the dark belt of fir-trees that skirted the eastern side of the Wifforde domain, I first heard that tale repeated right through, from beginning to end. My uncle did not speak harshly of either of my parents; he only pointed out the suffering and the regret his sister had brought upon herself and her family by her disobedience; and he prayed of me beyond all things to keep truthful, to avoid concealment even in the most trivial matters, to be honest and thorough.

"And if you will only promise me this, and try with all your heart and soul and strength to keep it, I shall not be afraid, even with your nature, to see you start on your journey through life, which you may have to perform alone some day—though not while I live, please God."

"I will try to be good, uncle," I answered. "I have tried; but I will try harder now, for poor grannie's sake and yours."

He took my hand and shook it, just as if I had been a man; and then we went back into the house together, and found my grandmother looking all the happier for that long talk with her first-born.

He stayed with us until the Monday morning, and we amused ourselves with long walks about the country—by nutting and gathering blackberries, and by visits to people he had known in his younger days.

Never, in my recollection, had one of my grandmother's sons paid her so lengthened a visit; and the dear soul was quite gratified at having a male creature to fuss over.

Marvellous were the culinary delicacies she prepared for his delectation. Wonderful was it to behold the thought she took for his comfort, and the means she devised to insure it. Sometimes my uncle would say to her—

"Mother, if I came here often, you would completely spoil me."

"My children have never given me a chance of spoiling them," she answered on one occasion; and there was a slight tremor in her voice as she spoke, the meaning of which I did not understand then, though I comprehend now that there are times in a woman's life when it does seem a trial to have reared sons and daughters only in order to give them over to the daughters and sons of other people, whose interests shall be their interests, whose hopes shall be their hopes, and who shall hold such possession of them, that in due time the old home becomes but a vague memory.

"Be very good to my mother, Nannie," were the last words he said to me; and then she and I, hand clasped in hand, went back from the little gate—whence we had watched his retreating figure till it disappeared in the distance—to the seam, and the knitting, and the stocking-mending, and the long-ago stories that had made up the tale of our usual existence, the not unpleasing monotony of which I have tried, scarcely so successfully as might be desired, to describe.

CHAPTER VIII.

MISS CLEEVES.

SKIRTING the Wifforde estate, that river from which our valley derived its name flowed sometimes quietly, sometimes noisily, on its way to the sea.

When the winter rains fell, and the drifting snow lay thick upon the green fields around Lovedale, then the Love dashed over stones and boulders, a very giant in its might; and again, when the ice under which it had perforce kept within bounds was melted in the early spring—then once more the waters had dominion over the earth, flooding the fields, undermining the banks, uprooting the sheltering trees, bearing huge rocks along in its progress.

In its strength the Love was a very lion, but in its gentleness it could be a lamb.

To hear its listless ripple in the summer-time, it was impossible to realize the roar and din of its December career.

Late on into the autumn it sometimes sang its low-voiced melody, and there was no time in the year that I loved its tones better than when, beneath orange and red foliage, daintily tripping its way around rock and stone, just covering the gravel and the sand, touching with a caressing hand ferns, brambles, and grasses, it dreamed its life away just as I was dreaming mine.

Dear river! I close my eyes, and in imagination I hear your ripple and lament, still the same as I heard it one autumn morning long ago, when I sat perched on a great stone in the middle of your stream, singing to your accompaniment.

Have I said the early morning was the perfectly free part of my life? If not, let me say so now. We were awake with the first streak of day, we breakfasted at unheard of hours. After breakfast my grandmother, unlike Desdemona in all other respects, was, like her, on household cares intent, and only too glad for me to find some employment or amusement that should ease her of my unprofitable presence.

During that period I was "somewhere" —all she then cared to know; in the garden, by the beehives, dusting the nicknacks, perhaps strumming the spinet. Latterly, however, I was a long way from home; singing where no one could hear me—singing to the birds, and the trees, and the murmuring river songs that mine own soul alone had thorough cognisance of.

We lose all this as we grow older. Men forget the mad passion with which they wooed Joan, and Joan on her side has only a faint memory of the throb her heart gave when she heard the gate latch lifted to give ingress to her lover. Artistes sing for so many guineas a roulade; artists paint for so many hundred pounds a face—perhaps *the* face—for such a number of guineas a landscape—perchance *the* landscape—with which a thousand enchanting or heartbreaking memories are connected.

Life seems to me so odd a thing divested of its romance, as mistakenly all of us try sooner or later to depict it, that in despair —looking at the whole scheme as that scheme is sometimes represented to me in the pages of books and the axioms of those with whom I come in contact—I must lay down my pen for a moment ere I can make the boulders and the stones, the overhanging trees, and the ferns and grasses of that wandering Love, mine again—once more.

There, it belongs to me, that past. It is the early morning of a day in autumn; and I, having followed the bend of the stream from that deep defile far below our cottage, where it flowed on swifter and darker towards the sea, up to the higher ground, found myself at length in a spot which always delighted my soul, filling it with a rapture and a peace that were none the less real because I never could understand the source whence they sprang.

It is the early morning, and the sun shines brightly. I sit down on a boulder in the middle of the stream, and look around on the beautiful earth. To my right are pleasant fields, sloping gently away to the valley below; to my left lies the gable of the Great House, seen imperfectly, by reason of intervening plantations. Against the bright blue sky the fir-trees stand out darker and more gloomy than ever. At my feet there is a pool of clear water, so clear and bright that I can see the gravel and sand at the bottom. Amongst the stones the river—by reason of long drought little more now than a trickling rivulet—wanders in and out, singing low songs to its own murmuring accompaniment. Under the alder-trees— mere bushes at this point—I can see the speckled trout darting hither and thither. The leaves of the trees are all yellow and gold, and scarlet and crimson; the low banks are clothed with brambles and ferns, with hawthorn-trees on which the berries are turning red; whilst on the mountain ash, or Rowan, as we called it, the rich clusters are already scarlet.

A glorious morning, with a certain crispness in the air, invigorating as the first breath of early spring; a morning when the autumn, having donned her best apparel, seeks to persuade one her mature beauty is greater than the timid loveliness of May, or the rich glory of August; seeks, and for the moment succeeds in her endeavour.

Basking in the sunshine, with eyes wandering hither and thither, I, at all events, am happy. Queen of all I survey, why should I not be so? For me the murmuring river, with never an uneasy thought as to poachers or rights of water; for me the distant church-spire, with no tithe to pay; for me the soft beauty of green fields sloping tenderly, with no rent to find; for me tangled brier and brilliant berry, without ever a halfpenny of wages to disburse; for me the dark plantations, and never a forester or gamekeeper to employ; for me the enjoyment of God's loveliest places, without rates, taxes, servants, appearance, to pay for.

Ought I not to be happy? Yea, truly; spite of my Fairport memories, or perchance because of them, I am happy.

Thirty miles stretch between me and Mrs. Isaac Motfield. Seated in the middle of the Love, she has no dominion over me.

If that beautiful lady came and talked to me now, Mrs. Isaac need never know anything about our interview. But then the lady was not in the least degree likely to come; and as I thought of that—thought vaguely that for the future the course of my life was settled, that I should never go to Fairport again, never behold any more the grand company I had once seen assembled within the walls of the Theatre Royal, never hear such singing more—my heart, spite of the crisp air and the bright sunshine, and the free wide landscape, died away in a sort of stupid faint.

Just then a thrush, perched on the dead branch of a willow close at hand, began to sing, quietly at first; but warming no doubt with his theme, unintelligible as the story might be to me, he burst forth ultimately into such a chaos of song, that when he ceased, I could not choose but follow him and *her*.

On his branch he sat and looked at me; from my rock I sang and looked at him; sang inspired by him and her, by the breath of the early morning, by memory, by youth, by solitude and beauty.

It was *her* song I sang. I had known it before, but re-learnt it from her teaching. Could I ever forget how she sang it? Never. As I write she comes forward to the footlights, and in her sweet foreign accents trills out that English ballad.

"Home, home," I sang, imitating all unconsciously her expression and intonation "sweet, sweet home"—the thrush turned his brown head on one side and looked at me intently, but uttered never a note—

"There's no place like home,
There's no—place like home!"

"Brava!" cried some one behind me at this juncture—"brava! encore! Don't in your excitement pitch yourself off that lofty peak. *Soyez tranquille;* I am coming to you as fast as it is possible, considering Nature has denied me the use of wings."

Yes, there she came, Miss Cleeves, attired in dazzling white, wearing a most remarkable sun-bonnet, picking her way over the stones to me—Annie!

"I say, little girl," she went on, "where

did you get that voice? Good Heavens, were I only the possessor of such a voice! You must have heard Madame Serlini. Oh, I remember now. You were the child in the stage-box who cried, as well you might, as I should have done had I dared. Sit down this moment, and sing that song for me again."

Here was a fix; I dared not refuse, and I could not obey. I essayed to do so in a sort of abject terror; but the words died away on my lips, and the tones of my voice were so low and subdued that the thrush, taking courage from my cowardice, broke forth into a triumphant carol at the end of my fourth line.

"There, you are a stupid!" exclaimed Miss Cleeves, as I broke down ignominiously. "I do hate shy people; they are such idiots." And sitting opposite to me, with her feet dangling over the pool, and her hands supporting her chin, she surveyed me at her leisure.

"Little girl," she said at length, breaking

a silence which appeared to me awful, "do you know who I am?"

"Yes, miss," I answered.

"Don't say 'miss,' like a charity-child; now, who am I?"

"Miss Elizabeth Cleeves."

"Quite right. And how do you know I am Miss Elizabeth Cleeves?"

She hurt my pride so much by mimicking my voice and manner, that taking courage I replied boldly enough—

"I have known you by sight for years. I first saw you standing on the balcony of Miss Wifforde's house at Fairport."

"So you have found your tongue," she remarked; "that is better. And now you will perhaps be kind enough to tell me who you are, and how it happens that I find you twenty miles from Fairport, sitting on a flat rock in the middle of the Love?"

"I live at Lovedale," was my answer; "in that small white cottage down yonder."

"Then how came you to see me at Fairport?"

"I was staying there with my uncle."

"And who took you to the opera?"

"Uncle Isaac. Mr. Bilbay gave him two tickets."

"What is your name?"

"Annie Trenet, miss."

"I told you before not to call me miss. If you do it again I shall box your ears. What is your father?"

"I have not a father."

"What was he when you had one?"

"He painted pictures."

"What sort of pictures?"

"Like that;" and I pointed vaguely to the hills and the trees and the rippling river.

"Oh, landscapes. Who was your mother?"

"Daughter of old Farmer Motfield. The Misses Wifforde bought his land when he died."

"Is your mother living? Why, child," she went on, as I shook my head, "your talk is a perfect obituary. It is like walking through a graveyard, and reading

'Sacred to the memory' at every step. If every one belonging to you is dead, who takes charge of you in that small white cottage down yonder?"

She was mimicking me again; but I did not care for it so much now. There was something in the mere fact of sitting on the same piece of rock, and talking on equal terms with a relative of the Wiffordes, which filled me with so terrible an astonishment, that minor matters seemed to fade away from view.

"I live with my grandmother," I answered.

"And who taught you to sing?"

"No one; and I cannot sing."

"Cannot sing!" repeated Miss Cleeves. "Ye stones, listen to that. If I could sing like that, little girl, I would do something. I don't know, indeed, what I would not do;" and she rose, and with arms folded across her bosom, looked solemnly down the stream as she made this assertion.

While she stood there a natural idea, suggested probably by her dress and general appearance, occurred to me.

"Miss Cleeves," I ventured, "do you think you ought to stay talking to me here? If the Misses Wifforde knew of it, they might not be pleased."

"Why not, child?"

She asked this moodily from under the shelter of her sun-bonnet.

"Because—because"—and the words almost stifled me, though I was determined to say them—"I am not a lady like you."

Then she turned and looked at me, took my measure from head to foot, from foot to head back again.

"Little girl," she said, "though you can sing as I never thought a child of your age could, you have a great deal to learn. Genius has made you a lady. Do you understand me?"

"No," I answered; albeit dimly I think

I comprehended what that remarkable young person meant.

"Genius has its own rank," she went on. "I shall come and see you. Good-bye; wont you shake hands?"

I felt timid about availing myself of her proffered courtesy.

"I wonder what will be the end of us both some day!" she said

O my soul, in the watches of the night I have often repeated that cry!

In the stillness her voice falls once more upon my ear; spite of the darkness that scene rises out of the past, and spreads itself before me in all the glory of an autumn morning, across which lay the glamour of my own young fancy.

Again the sun tips the many-coloured leaves with gold, again I behold the soft green fields sloping off gently towards Lovedale; there is our tiny cottage; at my feet ripples the Love. I stand alone on the boulder, while with light and rapid movement Miss Cleeves picks her way across the stream, and reaches the bank, and after one wave of her hand trips off in the direction of the Great House; and then I begin to pursue my own way down the stream, wondering in what words I shall tell my grandmother of that marvellous adventure.

CHAPTER IX.

I SING.

WHEN two persons who, so far as temperament is concerned, have not much in common live an utterly secluded existence, such, for example, as was led by us dwellers in the small white cottage, it is astonishing the difficulty that may be experienced by one at least of the twain in communicating the occurrence of any event which has happened out of the beaten track of every-day routine.

Along the monotonous road we trod anything in the shape of news was like some rare and beautiful flower springing beside our path; and yet, like a selfish little wretch, I should have preferred keeping the rare exotic, whose acquaintance I had made in the middle of the Love, for my own personal delectation. Besides, how would my grandmother receive the intelligence? How might I ever tell her that actually within sight of the Great House I had been indulging myself with a private concert, and singing " Home, Sweet Home," to the expressed satisfaction of Miss Elizabeth Cleeves?

That she would be shocked at my "boldness," I was well aware; that she would forbid me the Love and solitary rambles, I fully expected; that she would desire me for the future to "mind my seam," and leave singing to ladies and play-actors, were things of course. Nevertheless, I felt it incumbent upon me to divulge the secret; and after weary hours of waiting and consideration and hesitation, my opportunity came.

It was after tea; household duties were ended for the day. In the cowshed Cowslip was chewing the cud with luxurious industry; in the stable Tom had finished his oats and chaff, and was thinking of settling down for the night; long before the pigs had nestled underneath the straw, and now lay, snouts extended, snoring in ecstatic comfort; the hens, led by a patriarchal cock, had retired to roost some hours previously; and the ducks I had seen waddling up from their accustomed pond, while there was still light enough to show the green paddock, and the white procession defiling homewards to the music of an occasional "quack."

Within the house everything was almost as still as in the farmyard. Another Jack and another Jill made love in the kitchen, where previous vows had resulted in matrimony; in the parlour my grandmother sat, knitting stockings intended for the use of one of her progeny; while I silently stitched away at a wristband, destined in good time to walk about Fairport, attached to one of Uncle Isaac's snowy shirts.

There had been a long pause, broken only by the click of her needles, and the noise I made in drawing my thread in and out. I was considering how I should commence my story, and my companion evidently, after the manner of some elderly persons, resented my silence.

"Why are you so dull and quiet tonight?" she inquired.

"I was thinking, grannie," I replied.

"That is a very bad habit for you to fall into. You should break yourself of it."

"I will try, grannie," was my meek answer.

"And what were you thinking about?" she next inquired.

"About Miss Elizabeth Cleeves," I said, taking courage. "I met her this morning when I was out."

"Well, there is nothing wonderful to think of in that. You have seen her many a time before. How was she dressed? Was she riding with Mr. Sylvester, or in the carriage with her aunts?"

"She was neither, grannie. She was standing on a big stone in the Love talking to me."

Notwithstanding my dread of consequences, I could not help feeling a little triumph in noticing the effect produced by this statement.

Here was news with a vengeance; here was food for reflection and comment; here was "Startling Intelligence," inserted in our domestic newspaper; and all by me.

"Talking to you!" repeated my grandmother; "what in the world could Miss Elizabeth find to say to you."

To the speaker, it was evident she looked upon the announcement made so suddenly as she might at an assertion that I had met Queen Victoria taking a morning stroll through Lovedale, and been honoured by an interview.

"She asked me a great many questions,"

was my reply, "about my father and mother, and where I lived, and who took care of me, and how I happened to go to the opera at Fairport—she saw me there; I think she sees everything—and who taught me to sing. And then, when I told her I could not sing, she laughed and said she wished she had a voice like mine. She is such a strange young lady, grannie. She called me 'little girl,' and forbade my saying 'Miss;' and when I asked if she did not think the Misses Wifforde would be angry if they knew she was there talking to me, she laughed again, and said she meant to come here; and, oh, grannie, don't be angry about it, for I was afraid to say her nay."

I looked up in my grandmother's face, frightened by the unbroken silence she had maintained during this long sentence, and beheld there an expression I shall never forget.

It was as though she were bearing the

trouble of her life over again. After my own fashion, with that sort of sympathy which a dumb animal can afford to its master, I vaguely understood that the drama of my mother's flight, the tragedy of that short career, was being enacted on the stage of her heart once more.

"Grannie, grannie!" I cried in my terror, "don't look like that! Forgive me, and I will try never to sing again. I promised Uncle Isaac I would be good to you and everybody, and I will if I can, grannie."

We were locked in each other's arms by this time, and she strained me to her heart, as if she felt there was safety for me nowhere else in the world.

Then I heard her murmur—

"I see now my son was right. It pleases God to make those even of a family different one from another. May He guide me and this child!"

And all the while I, feeling there was something terrible in so strange a prayer, clung closer to her, and cried aloud—

"Please, grannie, don't. Oh, grannie, don't, please!"

But as if she had not heard, she said, putting me back into my chair—

"Annie, there is one thing I hope you are not—I am sure you are not—and that is, deceitful to your old grandmother."

"I am sure I would not deceive anybody, if I knew it," I answered boldly, my indignation checking the coming tears; for I knew what it had cost me to be frank with her, and this was the result.

"Then tell me, word for word, if you can remember, what passed between you and Miss Cleeves."

Her tone was so gentle, it disarmed me instantly. Yes, something underlay her anxiety I could not understand then, that I never did fully comprehend till I had children of my own; and so I began my narrative. No need to say "if I could remember." In lives like ours, the few incidents they contained were all we had to remember. How, therefore, was it possible for me to forget?

I told her all about it; how in the beautiful morning, in the middle of the river, all alone, as I thought, I was singing my song; and so forth.

There was no enthusiasm in my narrative. Perhaps it produced all the more effect for that very reason. When I finished, I knew intuitively I had made my mark.

One from the Great House, young though she was, flighty though she might be, had praised and recognised the poor ability I possessed; and every one who has learned the lesson of life from out the book of his own bitter experience cannot fail to understand that where there is any real ability, those of a man's household are the last to recognise the fact. For them uncrowned genius has no prospective monarchy. In their eyes the familiar locks would seem unreal burdened by the phantom laurel-wreath to come. It is always the unreal, the speculative, the self-asserting, that carries domestic conviction of its false presence with it; and so the actual genius lies dormant till some stranger, crossing the threshold, lays his hand upon it, or till genius, having crossed its own threshold, finds in the stirring world that recognition which was denied on the parental hearth.

Yes, at length, vaguely, sorrowfully, my grandmother understood I was a duckling who must, sooner or later steal away from the cottage and the familiar existence to the great lake of life.

To that my instincts tended. I was, after my fashion, artistic. I had a voice. Miss Cleeves said so, and the words were solemn to my grandmother as though spoken by an oracle.

I had a voice. Until that hour she never recognised the possibility of such a stupendous fact. The chicken she had reared, in fact, proved not a chicken at all, but a strange creature who could gyrate in unfamiliar waters, and talk without much embarrassment to Miss Cleeves herself.

"What did you say you sang to the young lady?" my grandmother at length inquired.

"I did not sing anything to her," I answered. "She asked me to do so, but I felt shy and broke down. What she heard me singing was Madame Serlini's ballad, 'Home, Sweet Home.'"

"I know the song," she remarked; "but I should like to hear it from you. Sing it for me."

At these words I arose, and going into the darkest corner of the apartment, thrice essayed to commence—vainly.

Then, in a sort of desperation, I closed my eyes. I reproduced the crowded theatre, the footlights, the beautiful lady; and just as if I were in my small way a *prima donna* in our atom of a room, I began "Home, Sweet Home."

I sang it with the whole of my little soul

in the work. I sang it as though pit, gallery, boxes, and stalls were hanging on my words in rapt attention.

I ended, and there was a dead silence. I opened my eyes, and from my corner looked towards the figure seated beside the round table, lighted by a solitary candle.

Her elbows rested on the table, her head supported by her hands.

I cannot tell what she was thinking of. Altogether I know it seemed more than I could bear.

Out of the room, up the few steep stairs into my small chamber, I crept silently to bed.

Long after my best friend thought I was sound asleep, I heard her praying audibly by my side, " Lord, keep this child from evil ;" but I could not tell her I still lay wide awake, both because I thought she might not like to know I was listening, and also because I felt that if I spoke, my own heart must burst.

CHAPTER X.

OUR VISITOR.

IT would be impossible for me to mark with either black or white pebbles the Sundays of that faraway time. But for the bees and the garden, the occasional lamb, the calf just weaned, the newly-hatched clutch of chickens, the budding leaves of spring, the perfumes of summer, the rich mellow hues of autumn, and the snows and icicles of winter, Sunday would, I fear, in our humble home at Lovedale, have proved a dreary holy time to me.

As it was, there comes wafted to me from those Sabbaths of childhood a sense of peace, of happiness, and repose. Through the great silence which always seemed to follow the stir and bustle of morning service, there break upon my ear the lazy murmur of honey-laden bees, the ripple of the Love, the soft bleating of sheep, the prating of our favourite pullets, the plaintive chirrup of a stray chicken.

And if my thoughts would sometimes soar off to Fairport and Fairport doings on Sundays, they always ended their flight in St. Stephen's Church, and resting with folded wings under the tablet aforementioned, sat listening with a trembling delight to the pealing organ, and the voices of men and women singing triumphant praises to the Lord on high.

There was no organ at Lovedale, either in the church—whither the Misses Wifforde drove in great state and ceremony—or in the chapel, where we repaired on foot with no ceremony at all, unless indeed our best clothes, which were donned only once a week, could be considered robes of state; and the six Psalm tunes that constituted our repertory utterly failed to satisfy the musical requirements of one now so critical as Annie Trenet, who had not only frequently stolen into St. Stephen's on Saturday evenings to listen to private rehearsals of the chants intended to delight next day a Fairport congregation, but had actually heard Madame Serlini sing, and been spoken to by her afterwards.

There are, I imagine, some children to whom, long before they can understand the meaning and value of forms and ceremonies, the service of the Church seems a more grateful form of worship than the colder service favoured by Dissent. It was so with me, at all events. The bare white walls, the square staring windows, the stained-deal pulpit, and plain whitewashed ceiling, contrasted unfavourably with the softened light, the painted glass, the arched roof, the old monuments that delighted my heart in St. Stephen's.

In our chapel there were no monuments;

there was only one hideous tablet, which exactly resembled a sheet of mourning note-paper. A rim of black marble edged a white slab, whereon was set forth this statement :—

Erected in Memory of
JOSHUA SANDELLS, ESQUIRE,
Formerly of this Parish,
And Founder of this Chapel.

He was an affectionate husband, a tender parent, a faithful friend, and a sound Christian.

He passed to his eternal rest on the 1st day of June, 1829, at his residence, Fairport House, near Fairport.

This tablet is presented to Ebenezer Chapel by his Widow, who mourns not as those who have no hope.

"He being dead, yet speaketh."

The service was as bald as the building: extempore prayers of an interminable length; hymns consisting of about a dozen verses, sung in unison by the whole congregation (myself excepted), principally through their noses; two chapters of the Bible, one selected from the Old and another from the New Testament, both of which our minister considered it incumbent upon him to expound; and a sermon—shall I ever forget those sermons, with their "thirdly," "lastly," "finally," and "in conclusion?"—that was the religious bill of fare presented to us Sunday after Sunday in Lovedale.

But yet it was a form of diet which the inhabitants seemed to like better than that offered in the little church hard by. The church counted its worshippers by tens, we by fifties. Living, the Lovedale people did not affect its precincts; dead, they dotted its graveyard. Under a green mound slept my grandfather and his fathers before him.

Two headstones placed side by side marked the last home of Motfields almost without number; and often on Sundays, indeed generally, when we came out of our Bethel, our steps wandered naturally into that quiet churchyard, where we were wont to stand silent beside one especial spot, whilst the sunbeams flitted in and out, playing at hide-and-seek amongst the graves.

When we got home again, we dined, and then our servant donned her best apparel, and went to afternoon service.

Regularly when the door banged after her, my grandmother was wont to place an immense family Bible on a little table drawn close up to the window, and she read the large print till she fell asleep; whilst I amused myself with the few books our shelves boasted that could be considered proper reading for Sunday.

How vividly I remember those well-thumbed volumes, in which, on the merest threads of a story, pearls of religious instruction were strung! *Mary and her Mamma* was the title of one of them; and if Mary only got one half so tired of her parent as I did, she must indeed have been delighted at the prospect of entering woman's estate. I liked some accounts of missionary work the best. In those books there was at all events some variety, some movement, some change of scene and people; but in *Mary,* when the mamma said, "I intend to walk across to Moor Edge, and call upon kind Mrs. Dorcas; would my little daughter like to accompany me?" I always knew a sermon was impending. There was a deliberate deceitfulness in those books which filled me with a profound despair.

It was like never having any jam that had not a pill or a powder lurking amid the sweetness. What a relief it used to be when my grandmother's eyes were fairly closed, and the large spectacles covered shut lids!

Noiselessly at that juncture I was wont to leave the apartment, and seek amusement, if it were fine, out of doors; if it were wet, in turning over my few quasi-possessions in the tiny room appropriated to my use.

Later on, when Hannah returned, we

had tea; and after tea I read aloud the *Pilgrim's Progress*, or that other progress of Christian's wife, which always seemed to me more charming than his own. Real to my imagination were the Slough of Despond, the path beset with dangers, the key which gave liberty to the captives in Doubting Castle, the wicked city where Faithful was put to death, the arbour where Christian lost his roll, the river broad and deep, and the city higher than the clouds, which, like Bunyan, I wished to enter, that I too might behold the streets paved with gold, and the men with crowns on their heads, palms in their hands, and golden harps, to sing praises withal, that walked therein.

I did not in the least comprehend in those days the true meaning of the tale. It seemed to me a real account of travels undertaken by real men, women, and children, who, after passing through great dangers, enduring much trouble, surmounting many obstacles, entered at last into a sort of fairyland such as was depicted in the story-books I at that time loved.

It is well, perhaps, to read Bunyan after this fashion when a child, since it invests religion with a certain "glamour," if the word be not profane, that it is impossible to throw over the subject at a later period.

For example, although my grandmother looked upon Bunyan's *Pilgrim* with a sort of devout awe only second to that with which she regarded the Holy Scriptures, nevertheless she went to sleep over the narration I regarded as so full of interest. To her the *Progress* was merely a good book; to me it was a story full of incident and excitement—a story so full, indeed, that I should frequently have indulged myself with a private perusal, had not such a liberty been tacitly forbidden by the fact of the volume being kept on the topmost shelf of a very inaccessible cupboard.

By some accident the *Pilgrim* had become possessed of a very handsome binding; and when we brought him down on Sundays, we were careful to keep the grey linen in which his morocco binding was swathed close round the book, lest a chance touch should damage the outer garment, that my grandmother considered as second only in importance to that in which he was clothed in a better world at the end of his journey.

Worn and frayed is that binding now; the leather has lost the glory of its first youth, the gilding is tarnished, the pages are discoloured; but the story the text tells is dear to me as it was when I sat in our little parlour and read that ever-new tale aloud.

An uneventful life to chronicle, an existence almost devoid of incident, and yet perhaps for that reason the few events that occurred seemed very remarkable and very grateful to our monotonous experience.

Our mental appetites had never been surfeited with a perpetual feast of exciting surprises. To us the daily gossip, the latest scandal, the visits, the letters, and the news of ordinary society were as foreign as rich soups, made dishes, curious puddings, and French confectionery on our dinner-table; and accordingly, when a *bonne bouche* did come in our way, we made the most of it. We turned an incident, as the old dissenting minister is reported to have turned Ephraim, inside out, upside down, round and about; but it was generally a long period before we followed the preacher's final example, and turned our subject, as he did Ephraim, about his business.

My short youth is a wonderful period now to look back upon. Counted by years, I know it was brief indeed; and yet to my memory that time of sweet repose, of dreamy idleness, of happy innocence, lengthens itself out to a century at least.

What is twelve months of life, when life begins to seem precious to us—a thing desirable to have and to hold.

The days from Christmas to Christmas I feel now able to clasp in my hand. Spring is but a whiff of hawthorn-blossoms passed under my nostrils, and then fading away to make room for the roses of summer. And what are they to me? In comparison to the rose-days of my childhood, they seem but a momentary blaze of beauty.

What are the fruits of autumn—the gorgeous tints with which she paints each leaf and berry? Alas, alas! when we have sat at Nature's table month after month and year after year, one cannot bring to the feast that keen enjoyment which gave such a relish to existence when all the world was young, when others took all the care and trouble and anxiety on their shoulders, and worldly sorrows were as unknown to the little ones as worldly hopes.

So far my life had been tranquil as the

quiet beauty of Lovedale; but a change—not a sharp or painful change, albeit it was unexpected—chanced to be close at hand.

How well I remember each trifling detail of that Sunday afternoon when it came! We were sitting, after our usual fashion, in a little room that commanded a view of the Great House. Close drawn up to the window were chair and table for my grandmother's special benefit. The hearth was swept clean; for although the sun shone brightly out of doors, still within, the weather was chilly, and a fire acceptable. On a footstool beside the old-fashioned brass fender, which it almost scorched my hand to touch, I sat reading, longing all the while to be out under the golden-pippin tree, where I was well aware there were plenty of apples to be had for the trouble of picking them from the ground.

But my grandmother kept obstinately awake, and her prejudices were against wandering about the garden and eating fruit in the open air on Sundays. So, forced to bide my time, I remained quiet.

Once more I look round that silent room. There is the old harpsichord; above it hangs my mother's portrait. Large oil paintings by my father ornament the walls. There are dark oaken chairs, with quaint backs, and ornamented with much carving. There are shells from foreign shores; there are feather fans made by Indians; ivory trifles, brought no doubt by some sailor relative from China.

The history of those nicknacks—so alien to the modes and habits of the Motfields—which came from the cottage where my father died, I shall never know. For me they had always a singular fascination, and on that special afternoon, wearied of reading, I turned and contemplated with a new interest the curious but by no means valuable contents of our room.

How long I had sat there, weaving fantastic histories out of shells, fans, and pagodas, I cannot tell, when my grandmother's voice roused me from my dream.

"Annie, Annie, make haste!" she exclaimed, speaking quickly and suddenly. "Who is this coming here? Lor' o' mercy, girl, it is Miss Cleeves! Whatever can she want?"

As to what Miss Cleeves might or might not want, that young lady left me no time to speculate; for even before my grandmother had finished speaking, a prolonged knock echoed through our tiny house—a knock sufficient, so it seemed to me, who had never heard the like before, to bring the small tenement about our ears.

"Shall I go to the door?" I asked, turning cold and hot in the same second.

"Of course. We must not keep the young lady waiting."

And it was as well we did not; for before I could reach the door, she had her hand on the knocker again.

"Oh, there you are!" was her greeting.

"I thought you were all asleep. People do sleep at all sorts of times in the country. I should, if I lived in the country altogether. May I come in? If I may, don't stand looking at me as if I were an apparition. If I may not, be good enough to say so."

I opened the door wide, and she accepted that act as invitation to enter. Happily she could see the parlour, and my grandmother sitting there, the moment she set foot inside our habitation, or I do not know how I should ever have asked her to walk in.

As it happened, she stepped briskly forward and greeted my grandmother, who rose from her seat as she advanced.

"You are Mrs. Motfield, I suppose," said Miss Cleeves, holding out her hand, which my grandmother took as if she did not know what to do with it. "I want you to let Annie come out with me for a little while. She would, perhaps, like to see the gardens at the Great House, and there are none of the men about on Sundays—not at this hour. May she come?"

I looked at my grandmother—she was, I knew, full of objections; she was considering how she should state them. If Miss Cleeves had given her time, I should never have seen those wonderful gardens; but Miss Cleeves did not give her time. Miss Cleeves repeated her request before my grandmother had, figuratively speaking, drawn her breath.

"I do not know, Miss Cleeves, what to say," she hesitated. "Would your—would the Misses Wifforde——"

The woman who deliberates is lost. My grandmother had deliberated, and was lost.

"Would my respected relatives object to my taking a Sunday walk 'abroad with Sally?'" interrupted Miss Cleeves. "Certainly not. They are darling old souls; but if they began to object to my doings, I should pretty soon leave them and return to my mother, who is not a darling at all. Now, Miss Annie, if you mean to come with me, run upstairs and put on your bonnet, and let us be off. Oh, you are not sure whether you may or may not! She may, madam, is it not so?"

She had all the assurance of fifty years of age, and, when she chose to assume them, the grand airs of the *ancienne noblesse*. That last clause in her sentence, and the tone in which it was uttered, settled the matter, and enabled us both to understand the nature of the dominion she exercised over our ladies at the Great House.

"You can go, Annie, if—if—you would like to do so," said my grandmother, looking at me piteously; but I was too young to take up the weapons she laid down with much success.

"You will want me at home, grannie," I answered. I could not now put my own desires so far out of sight as I did in that sentence; but then I was under subjection, which, perhaps, detracts from the merit of my self-denial.

"What a simpleton you are!" exclaimed Miss Cleeves, without giving my grandmother time to answer. "I know you want to come with me, and you know I want you to come with me, and you know Mrs. Motfield is not afraid of my eating you up; therefore why will you not put on your bonnet at once? She may put it on without any fear of a scolding afterwards?" This to my grandmother.

"I suppose so. I never scold Annie," was the reply.

"Perhaps Annie is so good a little girl as never to require a scolding," was the reply, which made me fire up in defence of my dearest friend.

"I am not good, Miss Cleeves," I exclaimed, "but grannie is, and she does not scold."

"What a charming grandmother!" answered our visitor. "What a delightful thing it must be where no one says a cross word to anybody! Now, child, are you going to keep me waiting all day, or will you put on your bonnet at once?"

"You are very kind, miss," began my grandmother, as I well knew, in respectful expostulation; but Miss Cleeves gave her no time to finish her sentence.

"I am not kind at all. I came here to please myself, and I want to take Annie over the grounds to please myself also. It is frightfully dull up at the house, and she amuses me."

This was a light in which I had certainly never expected to find the matter placed, but it chanced to be the very one most calculated to win my grandmother's consent.

"You had better not keep Miss Cleeves waiting, dear," she said, quietly; and looking at her in astonishment, I saw at once she had taken up my former impression, and thought the intellect of Miss Wifforde's relative was affected. "Will you take a seat, miss?" she asked.

The last sentence I heard my new acquaintance utter as I left the room was, "No, thank you; I hate sitting. How people can remain glued to a chair for hours together, I cannot imagine."

During the short time I was absent, she contrived to take a correct mental inventory of our furniture and other effects. She criticised the pictures; she was good enough to admire some of our ornaments; she would have opened and tried the spinet, had not she been mildly reminded that it chanced to be Sunday; she looked at the views from the window; and having finally exhausted our interior, was about to make her way out into the garden, when I made my appearance.

"What a time you have been!" was her remark. "I could have put on fifty bonnets since you went upstairs. Now bid your grandmother good-bye, for perhaps I shall never let you come back to her again." After which speech she took me by the hand, just as though I was only about six years old, and in this manner conducted me to the entrance gates of that domain it had been my habit, almost from infancy, to regard with a kind of holy awe.

CHAPTER XI.

I AM DECEIVED.

HAD Miss Cleeves given me time to enjoy myself, that Sunday afternoon's walk through those lovely grounds would have been one of the happiest of my life; but she hurried me so fast from lawns to gardens, from gardens to park, from aviary to lake, from summer-house to waterfall, that I could only carry back to our cottage a confused memory of trees and turf, and parterres filled with exquisite flowers; of an all-pervading scent of heliotrope; of hot-houses, where hundreds of bunches of grapes hung from the roof, while peaches clustered thick on the trellis-work at the back.

She took me into the conservatory, where

there was not a plant I had ever seen before; she dragged me away almost by force from an entranced contemplation of silver and gold pheasants; she scarcely permitted a moment to be employed in viewing the swans. Only once did she allow a decided halt, and that was under a mulberry-tree. There in an incredibly short space of time she ate about a pint of the fruit, and came away with her hands dyed violet, and her dress stained in several places with the juice.

"Lucky it is not a silk," she remarked, when I drew her attention to this fact. " Aunt said this morning it was getting too chilly for muslins; but I carried my point. I detest silk dresses; don't you?"

My experience of them having been limited, I was unable to give a satisfactory answer.

" I like dresses," proceeded Miss Cleeves, "that wash, and are clean again. What is the good of being in the country if one has to be got up perpetually like a stiff-starched frill? It is very well for old ladies, who do not want to run about and enjoy themselves, to be arrayed in all sorts of magnificence; but I cannot see why young people should be victimized with fine clothes; can you?"

My Sunday apparel having been always a trouble to me, I could agree with her on this point, and felt glad to do so.

"You must find it very dull living all alone with your grandmother, and never having a young person to speak to," she said after a pause.

"I do not care much for young persons," I answered; "the few I have known never made themselves particularly pleasant to me."

"Present company of course excepted," she said.

"Yes," was my reply; "I like the little I have seen of you very well."

"Very well, indeed!" she repeated, laughing. "There is an ungrateful wretch, after all the trouble I have taken on your behalf. The least you might have said was that you liked me very much."

"But, Miss Cleeves," I expostulated, "you told my grandmother you did not take all that trouble to please me, but to please and amuse yourself."

"Ah, that was only my amiable way of putting it," she remarked, carelessly. "When you are as old as I am, you will not think of taking everything *au pied de la lettre.*"

"What does that mean?" I inquired.

"Why, you little dunce, do you not understand half a dozen words of the simplest French?"

I felt my face burn and my eyes fill with tears at her insolence, but I answered bravely enough—

"What chance have I ever had of learning anything?"

For a moment she remained silent, then

giving my hand a swing backwards and forwards, she said—

"That was a very rude speech of mine, and I beg your pardon. I am sorry to have vexed you."

"You did not vex me—much," was my answer; "but I have often and often wished I knew more."

"Yes," she replied, and walked on without speaking for a little time. Then she turned to me abruptly, and began, "What does your grandmother intend to do with you?"

"She does not intend to do anything with me that I know of."

"Does she not mean to have you properly educated?"

"She thinks I have learned all it is necessary for a girl in my station to understand."

"And what is that 'all,' if I may inquire?"

"I can read, and write, and do accounts;

I can sew pretty well, and could knit stockings, only grannie likes best to knit them herself; I am able to make bread, and butter. I do not think I have learned anything else."

"And I suppose ultimately your grandmother will want you to marry some respectable young man whose dairy you can look after, besides attending to his comfort and welfare generally."

"I have not heard grannie say anything about it; but I am sure she would be vexed if I ever married a man who was not respectable."

"What a funny child you are!" exclaimed Miss Cleeves; "funny old-fashioned little monkey! It is a blessing people are so differently constituted. Had I your voice, not all the grandmothers, mothers, and aunts in England should keep me in Lovedale an hour. I would go and make my way in the world, ay, even if I had to sing about the streets, till somebody recognised my gift and took me by the hand."

"Hush, hush!" I cried, for her vehemence frightened me. "What can you want more than you have now?"

"What have I?" she asked.

"All these beautiful gardens, all this lovely place. You have a grand house, you have carriages and horses."

"They are not mine," she said, sullenly.

"They are as good as yours," I answered, with for me considerable spirit, as I considered she was underrating her advantages and depreciating the Misses Wifforde's kindness. "They are as good as yours. This place is as much your home as our little cottage is mine. You can walk about and pull the flowers, and eat the fruit, just as I do, and some day you will marry Mr. Sylvester and be mistress here."

"Yes, that is the programme," she observed.

"And you will be quite happy, then."

"Assuredly," she agreed, with a covert smile which belied her words. "When I am married to Sylvester, and when I am mistress here, I shall be quite happy, no doubt."

"You puzzle me," I said.

"How shocking, how sinful to puzzle that dear wise little head of yours! I believe one of my earliest exploits was crying for the moon—in some shape or other I have been crying for the moon ever since."

"But what is the good of crying, if crying wont get a thing?"

"My mother would tell you—— But there, let us talk about something else. Come into the house, I want to show you my piano."

At this suggestion I drew back appalled. With much fear and trembling I had already followed her amongst many head of horned cattle; I had been knocked down by a huge dog; I had even ventured after my guide into the stables, and accepted her peremptory invitation to enter the loose stall tenanted by Mr. Sylvester's favourite horse.

"They are all as quiet as kittens," explained Miss Cleeves; "indeed, the carriage horses have no more spirit than old cats;" and by these and other assurances she had seduced me into dangerous proximity with creatures that had hind legs and stood seventeen hands high. But follow my leader any farther, I dared not.

Lured on by a certain fascination I had, with a shrinking trepidation, allowed myself to be led into the stable-yard, from which I could see many windows that looked out from the back of the Great House; but the thought of entering the house itself appalled me.

What if Miss Wifforde saw a stranger within her gates? what if already she had seen me? As the idea occurred, I tried to pull my hand away, with some dim idea of rushing off into the pine wood and secreting myself there. We were under the shadow of the pine branches when Miss Cleeves made her suggestion, and escape at the moment seemed easy and desirable. But my companion was stronger than I.

"No, my dear," she said, tightening her hold; "you are my prisoner, and I shall not let you away till it suits my sovereign will and pleasure; you remember I told your grandmother that possibly she might never see you again. There is a place for hanging up dresses in my bedroom as large as Red Rover's box; I think I shall shut you up there, so that I can lay my hand on you whenever I want some one to talk to."

I was not afraid of being locked up, but I was afraid of meeting any person.

How I besought the girl to let me go! how, even with tears, I begged and prayed of her to release me! But she only laughed at my entreaties; and when at length I threw myself on my knees before her, she laughed still louder.

The advantage was all on her side. She was not merely older and stronger than I, but she was a vixen in her strength. She did not care whether she hurt me or not; I dared not have hurt Miss Cleeves.

"You horrid obstinate little wretch," she cried, her eyes sparkling with fury; "I wonder at your presuming to set up your will against mine. Will you come into the house this moment, as I desire you? I shall beat you if you try my temper any longer. And besides, what is the use of your struggling? You know if you kicked, or scratched, or bit me, I could have you sent to prison, and fed on bread and water. You are a nasty ungrateful little thing; I wanted to be friends with you, and this is the way in which I am treated in return."

Blinded with tears and fairly conquered, I listened to this graphic *resumé* of my sins, and then endeavoured to effect a compromise.

Would she promise to let me leave the instant I had seen her piano? Would she insure that I should not meet her aunts or Miss Hunter, or anybody? Would she allow me to run home by myself through the dusk fast, because my grandmother must be getting uneasy?

All this I asked, and to all of it she replied—No! She refused to promise anything but this—that if I would not do what she asked, she would never forgive me; she would never speak to me while she lived again.

"And I will tell my aunts what a wicked girl you are, and they will not let you stay in their cottage," she finished; and then, when I reluctantly agreed to accompany her, she broke into a peal of laughter, and said—

"What a goose you are!"

It was therefore by reason of gross intimidation that I entered the Great House. To my intense relief the front door stood open, and we entered and passed through the hall, which was unlighted, without meeting any servant. Miss Cleeves, still suspiciously keeping hold of my wrist (it was black and swollen for a fortnight afterwards), led the way up four steps, broad and easy, then along a wide corridor, at the extreme end of which she opened a door, and signing me to enter, I stood next moment in the presence of Miss Laura and Miss Dorothea Wifforde.

Consider my feelings. Never had I been so terrified before ; not even when at St. Stephen's I had crept one Saturday evening into the dark church to listen to a rehearsal which was being held by the light of dips in the organ-loft, the form that I intended to sit down upon tipped over with a noise sufficient to bring organist and choir to a standstill, and to cause me to flee out into the graveyard as though a thousand ghosts were in hot pursuit. Never before—not when Mrs. Isaac Motfield opened her vials of wrath, and poured them over my devoted head—had fear taken such absolute possession of me, body and soul. No street Arab suddenly dragged from his accustomed gutter, and accorded the unwished-for honour of an interview with his temporal lord—the lord of a year—could have experienced one-half the agony that fell to my lot when introduced by that faithless and perverse girl into such high and mighty company.

There, at the entrance of a large room— a room so large indeed that to look down it seemed to me like looking down the main aisle of St. Stephen's—lighted, and that only dimly, by a smouldering wood fire, stood I, Annie Trenet, with Miss Cleeves, a heavy oaken door possessed of an immense handle, a long corridor, four steps, a wide hall, another door which my companion had closed on her entrance, more steps, an avenue apparently interminable, and the lodge gates, between me and liberty.

At the other end of the room sat the Misses Wifforde and Mr. Sylvester. On a table beside Miss Laura stood a hissing urn. They were not prepared for or expecting visitors even in their own rank of life. I knew how solemn a matter the entertainment of an invited guest was in our humble home, how utter the dismay when an uninvited one appeared at our doors. The solemnity and the dismay I mentally intensified after the fashion of a rule of three.

Given that the arrival of an unwished-for visitor caused a certain amount of annoyance and confusion in the Motfield household, what would it do in the Wifforde?

Never before did I cast out a sum so rapidly; and the result was—led on and deluded by Miss Cleeves, I had sinned past hope of pardon.

Too young still to find relief in strong phrases, I did not even whisper to myself, "God forgive her, for I cannot;" but I know I felt some sentence of that sort.

Here will the reader pardon a digression? Since I have arrived at years of discretion, the conclusion has been forced upon me, that when the period of strong feeling is well-nigh ended, that of strong expression commences; once we begin the tragedy of words, the tragedy of sensation must be a story of old. Which all, no doubt, will seem like nonsense-writing, for so quiet a tale as that of my poor life. But everything is comparative; and from my youth upwards the Misses Wifforde had bounded the limits of my social horizon, therefore the bating of breath and the quickening of pulse that occurred at the moment may perhaps be imperfectly understood, can certainly not be described.

It may be thought that, spite of doors and corridor, I might have fled even then.

But to me flight was impossible; I stood rooted to the carpet, whilst I heard, as in a dream, a voice asking—

"Where have you been, Lizzie? Sylvester went every place he could think of to look for you, but without success."

"It is a great pity Sylvester gave himself so much trouble," answered Miss Cleeves, advancing towards the fireplace, and pulling me after her; "he knows perfectly well I am not at all likely to tumble into the lake or the deep pool, and that is about the only sort of accident that could possibly occur in such benighted regions as these. I have passed a very profitable and pleasant afternoon in showing Miss Trenet (Miss Wifforde, Miss Trenet—general introduction considered as effected) the gardens and domain of the Great House. Miss Trenet is much impressed by the beauty and grandeur of the Wifforde estate, and considers that 'of such is the kingdom of heaven.'"

The fire was low, and Miss Wifforde

short-sighted, therefore she had not the slightest chance of recognising me, even supposing she had in her drives to and fro chanced to become aware of the fact of my existence.

"How do you do, my dear?" she said therefore in the kindest manner imaginable, extending her hand as she spoke. "I cannot at the moment recall to my mind where I have heard the name of Trenet before, but it sounds familiar. I hope your grandmamma's rheumatism is better."

"Thank you, ma'am," I answered, perfectly bewildered at this reception, "she is pretty well."

"I am glad to hear that," was the reply. "I feared from your grandpapa's manner this morning that it was rather a serious attack."

"Gracious goodness, aunt!" here interposed Miss Cleeves, "you do not suppose, surely, I should have devoted a whole afternoon to that horrid little girl the

Rawlings have imported. This creature is a discovery and possession of my own. I have stolen her as the fairies steal babies. She is nobody's child; and she lives nowhere in particular, unless it may be in the middle of the Love, where I made her acquaintance, singing like one of those insufficiently clothed young women who have no wardrobe to speak of, excepting a shock of hair and a looking-glass."

"Elizabeth!" exclaimed Miss Laura, in a tone of expostulation.

"Miss Laura Wifforde, my dear aunt, will you kindly pour out a cup of tea for this orphan child, whom I have adopted?" was all the notice that dreadful Miss Cleeves took of the implied reproof.

But matters had now come to a pass when I felt I must speak.

"I am very much obliged," I began— and my voice shook so painfully, that I had to jerk the words out, throwing each one singly, as it were, at my listeners; "but I would rather not have any tea, thank you—and oh, if you would let me go back to my grandmother! She will think I am lost; she will be so vexed at my having dared to come here."

"I declare, Annie Trenet, you are enough to provoke a saint!" cried out Miss Cleeves, before any one else could speak. "Everything was going on so beautifully; and you have spoilt it all. See if I ever take any more trouble for you again. You may stay at home for ever, and never see anything worth seeing, or hear anything worth hearing, for aught I care;" and Miss Cleeves was turning from me with an expression of anger and disdain when Miss Wifforde interposed her authority.

"Lizzie," she began—and by the flame that was licking its way round a log Mr. Sylvester had thrown on the fire, I could see she looked pained and angry—" in this house you *shall* pay some regard to the most ordinary rules of courtesy. Whoever this young lady may be, you have most grievously hurt her feelings——"

"And she has hurt mine!" interrupted Miss Cleeves. "I wanted to be friends with her, and she would not let me."

"Oh, Miss Cleeves, how can you say so?" I cried out. "You did show me beautiful things to-day, and I shall never forget them; and I am grateful. But—but—if I might only go home, ma'am"—this to Miss Wifforde, in utter despair of being able to finish my sentence as I had intended.

"Certainly, my dear, you shall go home," answered Miss Wifforde, kindly; "but first have a cup of tea and piece of cake, and then, if you will tell us where you live, some one shall return you safely to your grandmother."

"I can go home alone quite well, thank you," I said; "and I would rather not have any tea, please."

"What a strange girl!" remarked Miss Laura Wifforde, whilst Mr. Sylvester, looking on, said nothing, but glanced towards Miss Cleeves; and, as if in answer to that glance, she came across to the spot where I was standing with Miss Wifforde, who was standing also, looking down upon me in puzzled silence.

"Little Trenet," she began, "I have been very rude to you, and I am sorry for it. Let us kiss, and be friends;" and she suited the action to the words. "Here is a seat; take your tea, and I will tell my aunts all about it. One morning last week," continued Miss Cleeves, leaning on the back of an easy-chair she had pushed me into, and addressing her audience over my head, "while the other members of this household were wrapped in slumber—the servants here, I may remark, do not rise with the lark—I walked down to the river, expecting to find that pleasing stream as quiet and commonplace as ever. To my astonishment, however, as I neared its bank, I heard some one singing—not a subdued song, not after the fashion in which one generally hears words and music alike murdered, but out loud and clear, like a lark, or a prima donna, or a street crier, if you like that comparison better. My river nymph was seated on a stone in the middle of the stream, which rippled an accompaniment to her melody; and the ballad she had selected, and which she sang *à la* Madame Serlini, with long-drawn pauses and other thrilling effects, was 'Home, Sweet Home.' Although I did not in the least believe her to be anything but a spirit, I considered it my duty to applaud."

"Dear Lizzie," said Miss Laura, interrupting, "do get on with your story a little faster."

"I must either tell my story my own way, or not at all," answered Miss Cleeves.

"Could you not give us the outline first, and fill in the details afterwards?" inquired Mr. Sylvester.

"No, I could not. Shall I proceed, or shall I for ever after hold my tongue?"

"Proceed, by all means," decided Miss Wifforde, and Miss Cleeves triumphantly resumed her narrative.

"Where was I when you, Aunt Laura, interrupted the flow of my discourse?—Oh, clapping my hands and shouting brava *so* enthusiastically that my songstress jumped up, frightened apparently out of whatever amount of senses she possessed; I then recognised her as the impressionable small person who had wept so bitterly—why it is not for me to pretend to guess—when *Il Barbiere* was performed at Fairport.

"Of course I immediately inquired how it happened she had been transported from the stage-box in Fairport theatre to a great stone in the middle of the Love; whereupon she favoured me with various domestic particulars, stating, amongst other matters, that she was an orphan, the daughter of an artist, and that she lived in a white cottage down yonder with her grandmother, all of which, being interpreted, means that my nymph, when in the flesh and not in the spirit, takes up her abode in a certain picturesque dwelling on the way between here and Lovedale, owned by the Misses Wifforde, and tenanted by Mrs. Motfield."

"So, then," exclaimed Miss Wifforde, in the same kindly tones as before, only frosted —with the same amount of cordiality, only iced—"you are old Mrs. Motfield's granddaughter? I hope you will be a good girl, and try to prove a comfort to her; for she has known much sorrow."

How glad I was I had not tasted their tea or touched even a crumb of their cake!

Somehow, the fact of my abstinence enabled me to answer with more spirit than I had yet displayed, that "my grandmother often said she did not know what she should do without me."

"An observation which, incredible as it

may seem, I can vouch to be accurately reported," said Miss Cleeves. "Mrs. Motfield really cherishes the most touching faith in her grandchild's goodness; but you have not allowed me to complete my story."

"I think it is unnecessary for you to continue it," remarked Miss Wifforde. "We understand now who this—who Miss Trenet is; and if she will finish her tea, Thomas shall walk home with her, as no doubt Mrs. Motfield must feel uneasy at her absence."

"No doubt Mrs. Motfield feels perfectly easy in the matter," retorted Miss Cleeves. "I told her, as plainly as I could speak, that she need not be afraid of my eating Annie up. She knows the girl is quite safe with me."

"Nevertheless, my dear, as it is getting very dark, and as Mrs. Motfield probably keeps early hours, I think that if Miss Trenet——"

"I will not have any tea, thank you," I

said decidedly, interrupting the inevitable finish of her sentence I foresaw; "and I do not want any one to go home with me, please; and I am very much obliged for your kindness, Miss Cleeves; and — and good evening, ma'am," I concluded, hurriedly, wondering how I was ever to reach the end of that immense room—walk all over those intermediate yards of carpeting by myself.

"I am going to Mr. Rawlings," remarked Mr. Sylvester, quietly, "and will see that no harm reaches this young lady between here and the cottage, which I know by sight perfectly well."

"I will go with you to the parsonage," cried out Miss Cleeves.

"You have had quite walking enough to-day, Lizzie," suggested Miss Laura.

"Not one-half enough," she replied.

"I would much rather you remained quietly at home," remarked Mr. Sylvester, with charming candour.

"I know you would, and for that very reason I intend to walk unquietly abroad. Besides, I promised to return this lamb safe into the Motfield fold. Come, little Trenet; we will run all the way down the hill, and make Sylvester angry, if you like."

That was a mode of spending a Sunday evening to suggest under the very noses of the Misses Wifforde; and as they stood, with those noses rather uplifted in the air, too proud to wrangle with their relative, too proud even to interpose their authority before a stranger, I could not help feeling thankful that my lot had been cast in a cottage instead of in that immense house with those stately ladies, who looked as though they never could have been young, for guardians.

They were, however, too genuinely, after their fashion, gentlewomen not to endeavour, though vainly, to set me at my ease ere I departed from the Great House.

Of mine own accord I should never have

ventured a more familiar leave-taking than that previously recorded; but Miss Wifforde held out her hand, on the fingers of which diamonds glittered, and retained mine a moment while she said, "Tell Mrs. Motfield I believe her grandchild to be a good and modest girl."

While Miss Laura added, "I am sorry your feelings should have been wounded in this house, and that you would not take your tea."

Oh, that tea! But they meant it all kindly, those stately old ladies. They were very good to me, considering the circumstances under which I made their acquaintance.

Imagine, if you can (you being a humble member of the middle classes of society), a madcap young princess seducing you into the innermost sanctum of Windsor Castle, upon the privacy of her most gracious majesty Queen Victoria.

Whether the deed be possible or not,

my limited knowledge of such establishments does not enable me to decide. The reader is only requested to imagine such a catastrophe.

For my own part, kings and queens, emperors and empresses, were vague and impalpable powers, when compared with our ladies of the Great House.

Always in the future, when I heard that passage read in the Scriptures concerning those who were supposed to be drunk with new wine, I imagined they must have looked and felt as I did when, having just crossed the threshold of another life, I lifted my feet hurriedly from the steps, and thankfully retraced my way, still dizzy, still like one in a dream, to my humble home, which I fancied in my ignorance, I should never wish to leave again.

CHAPTER XII.

MISS CLEEVES' OPINIONS.

"SIL," began Miss Cleeves, when we were clear of the house, "did not the old ladies act 'more poker' splendidly this evening?"

"I wish you would not ridicule them, Lizzie," he replied; "you know I cannot bear to hear you."

"True, and I ought not to annoy you; but still, you must admit their backbones have been gradually stiffening into iron for innumerable centuries. Iron is not iron, but something else, in the first instance; and they, so long in process of stiffening, stiffened up into harder metal than ever when I introduced my protégée."

"And they were right to do so. I had

no business to go to the Great House, and you had no business to take me, Miss Cleeves," I answered. Out in the darkness, with the cool wind blowing upon my hot forehead, I was not afraid to speak my mind, and I spoke it.

"A miracle!" exclaimed Miss Cleeves; "little Trenet has found her tongue, and the power to use it. Go on, my dear. There is no evening service anywhere; and if there were, we should not attend it. In such and such a chapter, and at such and the twenty-four following verses, you will find it written—go on, Annie; the congregation has found the text, and is all attention."

"What is my text, then, Miss Cleeves?" I asked.

"Old heads shall be put on young shoulders immediately," she replied without a moment's hesitation; "for such is the law and the prophets."

"My dear Lizzie, how can you be so

absurd, and, I must add, so irreverent?" asked Mr. Sylvester.

"My dear Sil, the life we lead ought to make any young person absurd and irreverent. You, of course, are different, because when you came into the world the nurse found out you had already learned your A B C and Catechism. For my own part, I believe our respected Aunt Dorothy was born in a front, and had a set of false teeth in her cradle."

"You know," he interposed, rather vehemently, "she wears her own beautiful grey hair, and that there is nothing false about her."

"You need not get into a passion over the matter," she suggested; "I only spoke metaphorically; but I put it to you now as a matter of belief and fact: do you or do you not believe that when Miss Wifforde made her début on the stage of this wicked world, she was got up regardless of expense; with her hair quite smooth, and her clothing fitting her without a crease? My opinion is she came into existence beautifully dressed, and looking precisely what she does now—the primmest, stateliest, dearest, most provoking old lady in Christendom."

"Why provoking?"

"Oh, because she has a certain standard to which she would raise and lower all people. She cannot understand youth. Only to think how many hundred years must have come and gone since she was young herself! She cannot comprehend young people; she cannot comprehend me."

"You think that a very remarkable want of understanding?" He said this quietly, but I fancied I could detect a lurking sneer in his voice as he put the question.

"Yes; I am sure a child might understand me."

"I am by no means so certain of that," he replied. "What does Miss Trenet say?"

"I think it is very easy to understand Miss Cleeves," was my answer, finding one expected.

"You sweet darling! and what do you understand about Miss Cleeves?" coming round to the side on which I was walking, and putting her arm round my neck.

"I think you like your own way, and are angry when any one else wants her way."

"Meaning you and me."

"Meaning you and anybody." I said this bravely.

"There's a little rustic for you, Sil," remarked Miss Cleeves after a pause, which I know now was one of mortification. "There is your simple country maiden. If she be so caustic in her teens, what will she prove at thirty?"

"That is a problem I really cannot solve," replied Mr. Sylvester; and for a few minutes we all walked on in silence.

Then the young gentleman, wanting perhaps to soothe the trouble he knew I must have felt that evening, began to talk to me about myself and my home.

More especially, I remember, he spoke concerning music like one who loved it; and when the young moon was rising over the plantations of the Wifforde domain, I told him I never heard or imagined anything like Madame Serlini's singing; at which statement he smiled and said—

"You are not singular in your opinion. Some of the best musical critics of the day believe there never has been, and never will be, such another prima donna as Lucia Serlini, and I am inclined to agree with them. But you have a wonderful voice yourself, my cousin reports," he went on; "what do you intend to do with it?"

"I, sir? Nothing," was my answer.

How I was growing to hate my voice, which seemed always getting me into scrapes! If I could have buried it in the deep pool that night, it should never have prepared fresh troubles for me.

"Adhere to that resolution," he said, "and you will do well."

"Nonsense!" exclaimed Miss Cleeves; "she will make the best of that wonderful gift which God has given her, or do very ill. Suppose we had talents, Sil—or enough talent to make those we possess available—should we not turn them to account?"

There came no answer to this. Looking at the pair stealthily, as we three walked soberly along the road, I vaguely understood that they were unhappy; that the bread of dependence—be it ever so thickly spread with butter—must of necessity seem dry and tasteless in the mouths of some who have to eat it day by day.

Just as I had refused my tea and cake that night, so would they have refused some portions of their entertainment had they dared.

Somehow in my head there took root at that moment an idea that life is not so out of proportion as we are apt in our ignorance to think it. Early or late, one must begin to learn the letters of the social alphabet, with the view of reading the truths of our existence aright.

My first introduction into grand society commenced that curious process of education which, as it can never be considered quite ended until some one closes our eyelids for us in the last sleep earth knows, may not, I think, inappropriately be termed the education of hereafter; since having been going on through all time, it must somehow, for good or for evil, influence eternity.

As we neared the cottage I could see my grandmother standing by the gate, watching evidently for me. She had a shawl wrapped round her head and shoulders, so I knew she must have been standing there for a considerable period.

"Oh, Miss Cleeves," I cried, my conscience smiting me for having caused that dear old woman a moment's anxiety, "grannie is out waiting for me—see!"

"Don't be afraid," answered the young lady. "It was all my fault; and when I tell her so she will not be angry."

"She is never angry with me; I told you so before," I replied, a little rudely; "but she must have been uneasy or she would not be standing there, and I cannot bear to grieve her."

Hearing which, Miss Cleeves and Mr. Sylvester exchanged glances, and the latter said—

"Suppose you run on and tell her you have come back safe and sound. We shall not be more than two minutes after you."

No sooner said than done. Along the moonlit road I darted like an arrow released from the bow. Oh, what a sense of freedom seemed to enter my soul as I sped on, cleaving the crisp air of that clear bright autumn night!

I fancy the birds as they fly must feel the same sort of delight as I experienced. The noise made by my steps on the sandy road, slight though it was, quickened me to more rapid motion, and my breath came fast as, throwing my arms about her neck, I panted out—

"It is I, grannie; so glad to get back to you at last."

"Where have you been all this time, child?" she asked. "I could not rest indoors, thinking that something had happened to you. Where have you been?"

"At the Great House," was my answer. "I could not get away earlier. Miss Cleeves and Mr. Sylvester brought me home."

"Brought you home! You are dreaming. Brought you home, indeed! What next, I wonder!"

"I hope you have not been uneasy about Annie, Mrs. Motfield," cried Miss Cleeves, now distant about a dozen yards; "you remember I promised to bring her safe back to you, and here she is."

"You have taken far too much trouble, Miss," was the reply, "far too much. My duty to you, sir."

This to Miss Cleeves' companion, who raised his hat to my grandmother as though she had been a duchess.

"How deliciously sweet the flowers smell here!" exclaimed Miss Cleeves, inhaling the odours of our humble parterre as though they had never a plant or shrub in the whole of the Wifforde domain.

"Do not they smell as sweet at the Great House?" Mr. Sylvester inquired.

"No, I think not," was the reply. "One always meets with flowers in a small garden that are never to be found in a large one—I have often remarked that fact; but Mrs. Motfield's is altogether the dearest little house I ever saw in my life."

"Would you be pleased to walk in, Miss, and rest for awhile?" asked my grandmother.

I saw she did not like making the proposition lest she should seem taking a liberty, but she liked less the notion of appearing inhospitable.

"Yes," answered Miss Cleeves, "it would please me very much indeed, if I should not be in your way. If you are going to those tiresome Rawlings, Sil, you might call for me as you return, or you can come in if you choose."

"What does Mrs. Motfield say?" he asked, with a pleasant smile.

"I shall only be too much honoured, sir," she replied; and accordingly we all four entered the house, and passed into the sitting-room, which seemed crowded by the unusual number of occupants.

"Is not it a darling cosy tiny morsel of a place?" cried Miss Cleeves, appealing to her relative. "Is not it a curiosity parlour? Would not Aunt Laura give her eyes for that old china? Dear Mrs. Motfield, where did you get those heavenly cups and saucers?"

It was a custom of ours—a remnant of superstition it may seem to some persons, a proof to others that we were, as I have stated, very low indeed in the social scale—always on Sundays to wear and use the best of everything we possessed. Let the morning be ever so wet, let the sky be ever so murky, or the snow ever so deep, still, when we rose from our beds, we put on the newest and freshest of our clothes, we added some little dainty to our ordinary fare, we set out whatever of value or ornament our drawers and cupboards contained, we drank our tea out of delicate china cups, that had come from the far-away village where my father was buried, and it was poured from a silver tea-pot, which all the rest of the week we kept wrapped well up in flannel and locked carefully away.

It was therefore to very old and very beautiful china indeed that Miss Cleeves had directed her attention. My grandmother must have delayed the evening meal for my appearance, since the tray stood on the little table beside the hearth, and the tea had not, I saw, gone even through that solemn process known to us careful folks as being "wetted."

"You have not yet had tea," went on Miss Cleeves, as was her custom, without waiting for an answer to her question about the china. "Pray, Mrs. Motfield, do ask me to have some with you. Annie has not had a drop, though I stood guard over her on one side, and Miss Wifforde on the other, trying to make her swallow some. Sunday is the only day in the week we have no dinner; why is known alone to Providence and my aunts. The Wiffordes have some legend about the servants wanting to go to afternoon church—a total myth, I may remark by the way—and the consequence is, the moment we get back from morning service we are expected to eat a horrid cold luncheon, that is, I believe, laid out over night, as though it were a funeral feast, and we get nothing more, excepting a cup of tea, till nine o'clock, when we have supper—also cold—after which, and prayers, we are all very glad to bid each other good-night. The only comfort about the matter is, that the servants have to do with cold meat too, which I am sure is a serious trial to them."

So this was the way of keeping Sunday that obtained at the Great House. On the whole, I concluded our modest festivity and perusal of the *Pilgrim's Progress* appeared a more enticing programme.

Miss Cleeves, at all events, seemed to enjoy her Sunday evening in our little parlour; and even Mr. Sylvester, although she occasionally shocked his sense of grave propriety, could not always avoid laughing at her ceaseless chatter.

As to my grandmother, she listened, fairly amazed; not an idea, a prejudice, or an opinion of her life but Miss Cleeves knocked over like ninepins.

She sat there, dressed in her best black merino gown, with a pure white kerchief of fine lawn, clear-starched and ironed by her own hands, folded across her bosom, and secured at the throat by a brooch, set round with pearls, containing her mother's hair, with her white locks smoothly braided back under the high widow's cap, the fashion of which had never been altered in my memory, hearkening to this rattle-brained miss, who seemed to respect nothing in the heavens or on the earth.

She never spoke of the Misses Wifforde save as old darlings, or funny old things; she ridiculed the way in which the whole country-side fell down and worshipped before them; she called the Great House the High Place of Lovedale, and said the inhabitants thought it much more worthy of reverence than either church or chapel; she described the Lovedalites as being in matters of religion Catholics and Dissenters—both sects being disciples of Wifforde; she thought a London season would kill the poor dears, they would never survive, she declared, finding out, as a practical fact, that there were other families, richer, older, more remarkable than theirs; she inclined to a belief that if they had married fifty years before, and been blessed with twelve children apiece, a more intimate knowledge of the ways of young people must have ensued.

And all through the discourse my grandmother could not get in a word, even edgeways—no, not although Miss Cleeves ate more bread-and-butter covered thick with plum jam than I had ever seen consumed even by Tommy at Fairport, and drank her tea as though the old china cup imparted an extraordinary and delicious flavour to it.

The whole thing was like a dream, as much like a dream as my visit to the Great House, only more pleasant.

We felt far more at home with Mr. Sylvester and his cousin than had ever been the case when Miss Hunter favoured us with a call. He was so courteous, and she so lively. She told us all about her own home, and her relations; gave us a description of Dacres Park; favoured us with reminiscences of her early life; and imparted to my grandmother's astonished ears the intelligence that she was utterly weary of highly civilized stupidity, and that if she could choose her own career, and were possessed of any talent, she would turn ballad-singer, opera-dancer, or author before she would lead the monotonous existence most of the women she knew were doomed to pass.

Then, having finished her tea, and her general conversation, or rather declamation, she suddenly said to my grandmother—

"What are you going to do with Annie?"

"I do not exactly know what you mean, Miss," was the reply; while I pitifully whispered to Miss Cleeves—

"Don't, please; please, don't.

"Be quiet, you stupid little thing!" she answered, quite out loud. "I want to know whether you intend to let her voice waste its sweetness on the desert air of Lovedale, or whether you mean to have her properly instructed and brought out."

"I would rather not talk about Annie, if you will excuse my speaking so plainly," said my grandmother quietly enough, though I could see her face flush and her hands tremble. "She has been placed by God in an humble path of life, in comparison to yours, Miss; and I hope she will be content to walk in it honestly and discreetly, as her people have tried to do before her."

"Yes, grannie, I will!" I exclaimed; and what I said at the moment I meant.

The glimpses caught of the world outside my home had not seemed to me very alluring; my experiences of general society had not proved uninterruptedly pleasant.

Altogether home seemed to me that evening a very desirable place in which to dwell, my path in life a more congenial one than that trodden by the Misses Wifforde.

"There seems to be a delightful unanimity between you two," remarked Miss Cleeves, "as charming as it is novel. Nevertheless——"

"Lizzie," interrupted Mr. Sylvester at this point, "Mrs. Motfield has already told you she does not desire to discuss the question, and you should respect her wishes."

"That is the manner in which all mine are usually repressed," said Miss Cleeves, turning to my grandmother, and laughing good-humouredly. "Nevertheless," she proceeded, "I shall come and see you one of these days quite by myself, and you and I will have a long chat, with never a soul to bid us nay."

Had it been any other person but a relation of the Misses Wifforde who made this promise, I know my grandmother would have said she did not desire either her visits or her conversation or her counsel; but as matters stood, she was compelled to declare she should feel proud and happy to see Miss Cleeves at any time.

"*Cela va sans dire,*" remarked the young lady to Mr. Sylvester; and at the time I thought her extremely ill-bred for talking in a foreign language before people who could not understand what she meant.

I have heard the same thing done, however, so often since by persons who profess the very highest breeding, that I am beginning to doubt the accuracy of my judgment in that, as in many other matters of more and less importance.

Be this as it may, after Miss Cleeves' short French sentence, we all seemed to get a little dull; and I felt very glad when Mr. Sylvester told his cousin she must really think of retracing her steps to the Great House.

"It is too late for Mr. Rawlings," he

observed, as they passed out into the moonlight.

And Miss Cleeves answered—

"So far as I am concerned, I should always take good care it was too late for any of that delightful family."

And then we locked and bolted the door, and went back into our parlour. But we could not lock and bolt out the world which had stepped across the threshold of our secluded home that day.

CHAPTER XIII.

SHADOWS.

THAT "long chat" concerning me and my prospects which Miss Cleeves had left our house fully intending to have all to herself, ere many days were over, was destined never to take place. Unaccustomed to such eccentricities as standing for an hour at her garden-gate on a chilly night in autumn, my grandmother remarked next morning that she feared she had taken cold. Before tea-time she became worse, and went to bed early, observing that a basin of gruel and a sound night's sleep would cure her.

She had the gruel, but not the night's sleep. When day broke, she, who was always earliest astir in that early house, called to inquire if I were awake ; and on my answering her in the affirmative, asked for some water.

"I have not closed my eyes all night," she said, when I brought her a tumblerful of water cold as ice, which I had myself drawn from the picturesque well, arched over, and covered with moss, and ferns, and brambles. " I don't think I shall get up just yet, Nannie. I will turn round on my pillow, and try to have a nap. Kiss me, dear."

With a great sense of fear, none the less terrible because undefined, I obeyed her wish. Then I tucked the bedclothes warmly round her, drew the blinds across the window, stole to the door on tiptoe, and leaving it just unlatched, went downstairs as quietly as I could.

What an eternity that morning seemed to be! The sun, which had always before tempted me off to the river, or the woods, or the lanes, rose higher and higher, till I felt almost as though I hated his brightness. I went and talked to our then Jill about my grandmother's illness, which she treated as a light matter, adding—

"I told her she would take cold, wandering up and down that damp walk at her time of life, with nothing but a shawl about her head, and you see I am right;" which fact, I have no doubt, comforted her exceedingly.

Extracting but small consolation myself, however, from this proof of her prophetic powers, I sought Jack, whom I found in the cowhouse milking, his pail nearly full, and his shock head well planted into Cowslip's flank.

Him I informed that my grandmother had a very severe cold, and was unable to get up. Whereupon he remarked "it was a bad job;" and his conversational talents being few, our talk ended.

After this I fed the fowls, which were hungry and greedy, and fought and pecked each other in a manner that in my then frame of mind disgusted me. So I threw down the remainder of the barley in a heap, for them to scratch among and quarrel over at their leisure, and wandered off into the garden; where I plunged my hands into the beds of thyme, drawing my fingers backwards and forwards through the cushions of green leaves, ornamented with purple flowers. But the smell I usually loved so much seemed heavy and sickly, and I wondered how the great bees who came humming to their accustomed breakfast-table while I was standing beside the herb border could be so fond of that honey-laden corner. The bleating of distant sheep, the cooing of the pigeons, the very murmur of the Love, brought no pleasure to my heart.

I was out of tune; and, as is usual in such cases, the discord seemed in other instruments, not in mine own heart. I felt uneasy, not knowing why; and nothing in creation appeared to have a fear but myself.

I was unhappy, and yet all nature smiled and carolled as though existence did not contain such a thing as care. For the first time in my memory sickness and I had come face to face; and sickness, to those who have been accustomed only to behold health, is a mystery and a dread.

Strong were the dwellers in Lovedale, strong and hardworking; the hard work they did may indeed have been the principal secret of their strength. Small need was there for any doctor's services, save when children were brought into the world, or accidents happened, or little people caught childish diseases, or grown folk fell sick of that last illness which no doctor's skill is competent to cure. Now one dropped off, now another; the passing-bell, the freshly heaped-up mound, repeated to our senses the truth we were told every Sunday, that "man is mortal;" but to me sickness and death had hitherto been abstract questions, utterly outside my own experience.

In my memory there had been no mortal illness, no fight for life, no forlorn struggle with disease beneath our roof.

Into that quiet home no intruder had ever come with ready rule and hypocritically sad face, to take measure and instructions for the last narrow house man may occupy; no black procession had passed along the garden path, carrying something away which might return to the cottage never more; no mound had during my time been added on our behalf to those which already billowed the green turf of Lovedale churchyard. Save for the black-sealed letter announcing my father's decease, death and I had not touched garments even in passing. When therefore I beheld my grandmother, whom I had never before heard complain of any ailment beyond rheumatic pains, a sore throat, a headache, or any other slight malady, so ill that she called me to fetch her water, and then said she would lie in bed for a little while longer, I fell to conjuring up all sorts of sad fancies. She was ill, she was dying; she would die, and I had killed her—I, aided and abetted by Miss Cleeves.

I could not see the far-off village, my eyes were so dim with tears. I ceased to hear the humming of bees and the songs of birds, by reason of the rushing noise made by the waves of remorse, as they surged in upon my heart.

Some one—Jill—had spoken that morning about her age; it seemed hours and hours previously, but the sentence recurred over and over again. How old was she? to what age did people generally live? Threescore and ten, the Bible said—that was seventy years; but then our minister, and other ministers to whose discourses I had been privileged to listen, stated few attained to the allotted span, whereas in my own memory four of the inhabitants of Lovedale and neighbourhood had not passed away from the midst of friends and kindred till past eighty.

This question of the ages at which people die was not one which had hitherto engaged my attention—strangely enough, by the way, since I suppose very young people and actuaries of insurance offices are the only persons who ever really take an interest in the statistics of mortality—but I intended in the future to redeem my time.

If my grandmother got better, I would go down to Lovedale churchyard early some morning and count over all the headstones it contained sacred to the memories of those who had died over seventy years of age.

The registrar-general I now know would have told me that every record I found to this effect would reduce the average, and seriously and deleteriously affect my grandmother's chances of recovery; but I was unaware in those days that such a person existed, and imagined in my ignorance that if seven people had been able to live to ninety, there was all the more reason to suppose that another individual could do the same.

In a word, I concluded that what one man had done another man (or woman) might accomplish. Spite of registrar-generals, I am not to the present day quite sure that there may not be a substratum of truth in my theory.

By it, at all events, I proposed to test my grandmother's chances of long life.

Standing in that dear old garden—the Love rippling far below on its way to the distant sea, the scents of autumn flowers around, the accustomed sounds in my ears, before my eyes the unaccustomed sight of drawn blinds veiling sickness that might be mortal—the idea of life holding a future for me in which our cottage and its inmates might have no part, first occurred to me.

A world without a home, a time when I should have no place to run back to, no grannie to welcome me, no tender voice to chide. It came to my soul vaguely in that early morning, while the sun shone so bright. I was young, but old enough to cogitate matters which have puzzled wiser heads than mine. I was small for my years; and in some respects the growth of my mind had corresponded to that of my body. Some kindly influence, seeing the natural development, which might otherwise have proved unhealthy, perpetually "pinched back" the leaflets I tried to send forth; and the consequence was, that in comparison to other girls of the same age I remained without bud or promise of blossom. Sometimes when I see an experienced gardener nipping the young wood from off a plant that is making it prematurely, the time when I too was subjected to the same treatment recurs to me. All of sentiment, of fancy, of romance, of stretching forth, had been rigidly repressed; and yet at the first note of danger the sap of imagination rose within me, and I pictured all sorts of dangers, that were, like other products of imagination, destined to be realized in due course of time.

For imagination is only the reflex of things which have been, or the precursor of things which are to be. Looking back, it is plain to me now, that unwittingly I began that morning to untwist one of the tangled skeins of life.

Which may all seem high and mighty language to apply to the days of one's earlier girlhood; and yet nevertheless it is true, true as sickness, true as death, that I then contemplated face to face, and not on my own account, life's mystery for the first time.

What if grannie should be mortally ill, and die? I pictured in my own mind the darkened house, the parlour full of people clad in black, the something lying still and rigid with clasped hands and eyes closed, never to open again in this world; and worse than all, the long lonely afterwards—the mornings and the mid-days and the evenings without grannie, who loved me; and as I contemplated scene after scene of the panorama myself had painted, the whole thing seemed so real that, unable to endure the mocking sunlight and the intolerable solitude, I rushed into the house, and climbing up to the highest shelf of our parlour cupboard, took down the family Bible, which would, I knew, give me some reliable information concerning my grandmother's age.

She was not quite nineteen when she went to be the mistress of Motfield's farm, and therefore, once I found the date of her marriage, the matter became a question of addition.

There was the entry; made in a stiff, plain, yet withal crabbed hand, with ink which had scarcely faded through all the years of the time that had passed since then:

"Anne Boyson and Isaac Motfield, married the 16th day of August 17—."

Forty-five summers previously. To my youth what an eternity it seemed! Forty-five and nineteen made sixty-four. She was not quite sixty-four. Once some one told me about a man who lived to be a hundred and twenty ; *ergo*, my grandmother might still reign over her little territory for fifty-six years longer.

I breathed more freely. I wiped my eyes, I closed the family Bible, and gave it a hug ere replacing it on that topmost shelf of safety and honour. I had mounted on the seat of one of our old-fashioned chairs, in order to put it back carefully, when there came a tap-tapping at the window, which almost caused me to drop the book ; and looking round, I beheld Miss Cleeves arrayed in her habit and plumed brigand hat, rapping on the pane with her gold-handled whip, in order to attract my attention.

Never was vision more welcome. She looked the very embodiment of health and help.

I ran to the front door to meet her, crying as I opened it—

"Oh, Miss Cleeves, I am so glad to see you!"

"Are you glad really, little woman?" she said, taking me in her arms and kissing me. "I would not disturb you till you had finished your devotions. Do you generally perform your morning exercises out of that huge volume?"

"Don't laugh about things, please—not now," I entreated; "grannie is very ill."

"What is the matter with her?"

"I do not know."

"Good heavens! then why don't you send for somebody who will know? I declare, Annie Trenet, you have been crying; your eyes are red and moist, and your cheeks flushed and moist also. Tell me what is the matter with Mrs. Motfield this instant, you little stupid."

Thus exhorted, I repeated my former answer—I did not know, and I said so.

"At least you can tell me of what she complains."

If one did not answer Miss Cleeves' first question to her satisfaction, she at once assumed the air of a cross-examining counsel. After a fashion, she put one on oath, and then compelled a reply to it, "by virtue of that oath." It is a blessing I had nothing to conceal in those days, or I should, in Miss Cleeves' opinion, have committed perjury over and over again.

"She got a chill on Sunday night," I began; "she complained of feeling ill all day yesterday. She had some gruel——"

"Pah!" interjected Miss Cleeves.

"And could not sleep last night, and asked me early this morning to get her a glass of cold water."

"And I should not be in the least surprised if you have been crying your eyes out ever since, thinking she must be going to die. You foolish little Trenet! people do not die so easily as that comes to, more especially a strong hearty old lady like Mrs. Motfield. Make your mind easy about her, and if you cannot, take my advice and send for the doctor. I called to ask if you would walk up with me this afternoon so far as the falls; but now, of course, I wont say another word about it. Good-bye. I shall send down this evening to know how your patient is;" and putting her foot in the groom's hand, she was in her saddle before I could answer. "Good-bye, *au revoir*," she said, turning her head, and kissing her hand as her horse, with an impatient snort, started off full speed for home.

How pretty and graceful she looked! I can see the lines of her slight figure, the flow of her riding-skirt, the feathers in her hat, the gauntleted gloves, the tight trim linen collar, the red geranium fastened coquettishly in the front of her jacket, as plainly as I saw it that autumn morning.

Youth is so suitable to some people, it is a pity they should ever grow old.

After her departure I went upstairs to ask if my grandmother would like a cup of tea. She said yes; but still complained of illness.

"If I am not better in an hour's time, Annie," she remarked, "I should like some one to go for the doctor. I do not want a cold to settle down upon me at the beginning of the winter."

"Had not Jack better go at once?" I ventured to ask; and as no negative came, I sent him.

After that I sat down and wrote to my Uncle Isaac, telling him of his mother's illness, and stating I would not send my letter till I knew what the doctor thought of it.

What the doctor thought was ominous enough. He said that she had inflammation of the lungs.

Whether this was really the case or not is scarcely a question for me to decide. My own present impression is, she was not so ill then as he imagined; that whilst his treatment for a complaint of his own imagination brought her to the brink of the grave, the good things that came from the Great House during the course of her illness helped to restore her to strength. But in those days I accepted the doctor's opinion as final; and when Miss Cleeves remarked, "Inflammation! fiddle-de-dee!" I almost expected a judgment to follow her irreverence.

What a time that was, though! Upstairs lay the sufferer it had fallen to my lot to nurse—imperfectly it might be, but still to the best of my ability; whilst day after day her sons and their wives, and daughters and their husbands, kept coming and going, grumbling at and interfering with every household arrangement; requiring meals at unexpected and unreasonable hours; emptying our modest larder; criticising our management, and making me wild with vexation because they seemed to think me little better than a cumberer of the ground. All of them except Uncle Isaac, who boldly took my part and said—

"Annie is worth a dozen of some grown-up folks I could name; and for my part I feel quite easy at leaving my mother in her hands—that is, if the nursing be not too much for her."

"Oh no, indeed it is not!" I broke in; "I would do anything——" But here Mrs. Daniel interposed.

"Oh yes, we know all about that. According to your own account you are a miracle of unselfishness; but in my opinion you are a sly, underhanded cat, turning and twisting people who do not know you round your fingers. Look at your ingratitude to your poor dear aunt at Fairport; ah, there is nothing sharper than a serpent's tooth——"

"It seems to me," interposed my uncle, "that you are extremely unjust to Annie. What injury has the girl done to you or yours, that you should fly out on her like that?"

"Done!" repeated Mrs. Daniel, in a tone of supreme contempt.

"It is not my 'doing,' but my 'being,' uncle, which offends everybody," I exclaimed.

No matter what those present thought of me, I could not have kept back those words. After uttering them I went out of the room and the house, through the garden, and away to the extreme verge of the paddock, where, flinging myself on the grass, I cried till I could cry no more.

There Miss Cleeves found me. "Little Trenet," she said, "get up; look at me—speak." And when I would not obey her bidding, she sat down on the grass beside where I lay, and taking me in her arms as she might have done a child, said—

"Poor little woman, have they vexed you? Never mind; once Mrs. Motfield is well again, all will be well with you too."

And then I crept close to her with a sort of dumb appeal, and we two remained there in solemn silence for full five minutes.

"I think I am a great baby," was my first observation.

"I am sure you are," Miss Cleeves agreed with amiable alacrity; but she stroked my hair and patted my cheeks caressingly nevertheless.

What a time that was! what an amount of responsibility seemed suddenly thrown on my shoulders! How old I felt when, after having been up nearly all the night, I crept to bed, leaving Mary to take my place! How I blessed the minister's wife for coming up one evening when I felt quite worn out, and saying—

"Annie, this is getting too much for you. I will sit with Mrs. Motfield whilst you have a sound sleep."

How gratefully I stored up the memory of every kind word which was spoken! How I dreaded the visits of our relatives! How I rejoiced when, in dog- and market-carts and other vehicles, generally borrowed, they departed!

It came to an end at last. Before Christmas—thanks, as I have previously suggested, to the delicacies provided by the ladies at the Great House, who stopped their carriage at our gate three times, and sent on each occasion a footman to inquire how Mrs. Motfield was—my grandmother, aged considerably by her illness, but still, comparatively speaking, well again, came downstairs to her accustomed seat in our little parlour, and by slow degrees we fell into the old routine again.

One by one she picked up the threads dropped months before; little by little she resumed her wonted avocations; life presented its interests to her again; and save that the Bible lay open on the little table more frequently than formerly, and that we both seemed to have added some years to our age, there was no outward change to be noted in our existence. And yet I was conscious of an alteration in myself; I felt weary of the place, weary of my home, my occupations, my fancies.

I had shot up during those months spent

in a sick room, and outgrown, so people suggested, my strength. Perhaps physical weakness had some share in the depression and misery I felt; but I fancy mental sickness had more part in it than bodily illness.

Day was a toil to me and night a dread. Frost and snow, the Love rushing on in its winter might and strength to the sea, the early snowdrops, the budding crocuses, the first sights and sounds of spring—I had lost my love and relish for them all.

We found plenty to talk about, grannie and I, in the evenings over the fire; but the talk had no savour—the salt was gone, and the taste even of the most astounding fact insipid to me.

What was it to me that many of the ornaments wherein my heart once rejoiced were, when we came to consider ornaments again, nowhere to be found? I could not work myself up to a fitting state of indignation when we discoursed concerning a missing cream jug, and a couple of china bowls. If I could only have been assured that Mrs. Daniel and Mrs. Isaac Motfield would never enter the house again, if a bond had been possible whereby all the Motfields great and little, save and excepting my Uncle Isaac, might have bound themselves severally and collectively to keep away from Lovedale, the whole of the valuables I possessed should have gone to them without a word.

I hated my relatives as only very, very young people can hate—impotently, instinctively, totally. I hated to think of them, to utter their names, or to hear their names uttered. I had seen them during the course of that illness mentally naked, so to speak.

I had seen their greed, their sordid grasping, their envy and jealousy and uncharitableness. I had seen not, who could do and who give up most, but who could take all and do least. I had heard their bickerings and borne their taunts. I knew they grudged me the belongings that were mine of right, and to which they had not the remotest shadow of a claim. I was made to feel that in winning my grandmother's affections I had inflicted a wrong on them.

Cold were they, cold and worldly—men and women who valued money and plenishings, linen, plate, and clothing very high; who walked uprightly and respectably in the eye of the world; who were better, in their own opinion and that of their neighbours, than many publicans; and whom even I, with all my detestation of their ways and words and thoughts and habits, could not call sinners.

I know now their hearts, puffed up by success, were hard as the nether millstone; but I only knew then that, as I have said, I hated them with a hatred impossible to express in language.

For the first time in my memory, the sight of the primroses springing up on the sides of mossy banks, or showing their faces amongst the beech-leaves that last autumn's winds had strewed upon the ground, brought no feeling of gladness to me.

I walked about Lovedale listless and tired. The only thing I really longed for was a sight of the sea; but even if Mrs. Isaac would have had me at her house, I felt I could never bring myself to enter it again.

She and the rest of my kindred had shown me what tender mercies I might expect if I were left to their care. They had never believed my grandmother would recover, and they consequently, certain of the game, showed their hands too openly, as events proved.

Fortunately those were not days in which women of all ranks wielded the pen with the fatal facility of modern years, or I know not what epistles of wrath might not have been despatched from our cottage to those who had left it laden with spoil like the Israelites of old.

As matters stood, we talked of our losses between ourselves; but I could not evince that interest in the subject which it would have aroused twelve months previously.

Often my grandmother would put down her knitting, and, after looking at me over her spectacles, exclaim—

"I wonder what has come to you, child."

To which my invariable reply was—

"I am sure I don't know, grannie."

Shortly before Christmas Miss Cleeves had left Lovedale in order to pay a visit to her mother and her mother's relatives, the Dacres; so that our life flowed on literally without a break of any kind, except such as was supplied by a couple of letters written to me by that young lady from Dacres Park.

They were lively epistles, and it was kind of her to write; but I put them away, after they had been duly conned over by both of us, with a sense of depression which caused my grandmother to remark, that I did not seem to be glad to hear from Miss Cleeves; "though there are few young ladies in her rank who would take the trouble of writing to you all the way from London," she finished.

"Miss Cleeves is very kind," was my answer, "but I wish she would let me alone."

Could my grandmother have read my heart, she would have understood how intolerable the difference of rank between Miss Cleeves and myself had become. I was fit to associate with no one, I thought over and over again bitterly enough.

For my own people and my own relations, I did not care. What were their interests and likings to me? what were my interests and likings to them? On the other hand, how could I, Farmer Motfield's grandchild, ever expect to be regarded as an equal by one of the Wiffordes?

I had little education; of their ways I knew nothing; I was ignorant of their customs as of the rules of court etiquette. By turns Miss Cleeves petted and snubbed me; but she had been kind, so kind, during my grandmother's illness, that my heart clung to her with the same sort of gratitude a dog feels to some one who has been good to him.

It was spring again, and in her latest letter she announced her intention of returning to the Great House; "where" she proceeded, "my aunts, considering that I am in many respects still unworthy of the great dignity they have thrust upon me, propose that I shall have the inestimable advantage of a companion, able at once to direct my studies and improve my deportment. Fancy this! as if life at Lovedale had not been sufficiently insupportable before.

"Miss Cleeves does not seem very grateful for all the Misses Wifforde's kindness," observed my grandmother.

"Perhaps she does not think it kindness," I answered, hastily.

"Young people are not always the best judges of what *is* kindness," was the comment on this remark.

"Nor old people either," rose to my lips; but I did not utter so saucy a reply. I put aside my work, and looked out at the sunshine; and saying I thought I should like a walk, went into the woods, already fragrant with wild hyacinths, and white with anemones.

By the time I returned, it was the hour at which we invariably took tea; but to my astonishment the tray had not been brought in, and I beheld no sign of preparation for it.

Close by the window sat my grandmother, her hands clasped idly in her lap, her face graver and sadder than usual, her eyes scanning every flower in the garden, and steadfastly refusing to meet mine.

"Annie dear, Miss Wifforde wants to see you. She left a message for you to go up to the Great House at once. There is no need for you to change your dress; you can go as you are."

"What have I done? what is wrong? what does she want?" I asked.

"There is nothing wrong, so far as I know," answered my grandmother, "and I hope you never will do anything to offend Miss Wifforde; and as to what she wants, why, you can't hear unless you go to her; so the sooner you go the better."

There was a sharp irritability about the tone of this reply, different from my grandmother's usual quiet manner, and it struck me so forcibly, that I could not help saying—

"Are you angry with me, grannie, for anything?"

"Bless the child, no! Why should I be angry with you or anybody else? But run away now, or you will be walking in at their dinner-time."

Without another word I did as she told me, except that instead of running, I walked slowly all the way.

A woman opened the gates for me, and said, "Good afternoon, Miss," precisely as though I had a right to pass through them. When I arrived at the front door, the butler who answered my modest knock immediately allowed me to enter, and addressing Miss Hunter, who happened at the moment to be ascending the steps alluded to in a former chapter, stated briefly, "Miss Trenet is come."

To my great astonishment my lady's lady did not come forward to shake hands with me, as had been her wont during the course of the previous summer, when my grandmother and I chanced to encounter her on our way to chapel.

She only said, "Please follow me;" and I followed accordingly.

CHAPTER XIV.

MISS WIFFORDE MANŒUVRES.

THE only time I had ever previously entered the Great House was when enticed into it by Miss Cleeves; but my guide did not on the present occasion lead me along the gallery I so well remembered.

Looking back at intervals to see I did not get lost by the way, she conducted me up a broad staircase, then across a wide landing, and so into a passage, at the extreme end of which she stopped and knocked softly at the door.

"Come in," said a voice I knew belonged to Miss Wifforde; and Miss Hunter entered, leaving me outside.

"It is Miss Trenet, if you please, ma'am," I heard her announce; and then Miss Wifforde replied—

"Send her to me, and—you need not wait, Hunter; I will ring when I require anything."

"My mistress will see you," remarked the maid, who had, I thought, an inimical expression on her face; and she shut the door after me as if the room were a trap and the lock a spring.

Whatever it might be that Miss Wifforde had to say to me, I was bound to listen to it now.

There was nothing formidable, however, in the lady's manner. Seeing that I hesitated to come forward, she motioned me to do so, and touching my hand with the tips of her fingers, said, "How do you do, my dear?" with much condescension and intended cordiality of demeanour.

"My dear" replied she was quite well, believing an answer to be expected, though she has since had reason to doubt the fact.

"Sit down," went on Miss Wifforde, graciously pointing to a chair placed opposite to the windows; and I sat down, as in duty bound.

The truth is, I was for the moment bewildered, not merely by the frightful circumstance of finding myself *tête-à-tête* with Miss Wifforde, but also by the unwonted magnificence of her dressing-room.

Draperies, laces, old cabinets, inlaid tables, mirrors reflecting back the landscape, glasses in which I could see Miss Wifforde and myself reproduced at full length—these were some of the wonders I beheld.

Hitherto, the finest furniture of this description it had fallen to my lot to contemplate was contained in Mrs. Isaac Motfield's bed-chamber. Item, one four-post bedstead, upholstered in stiff crimson moreen, trimmed with black velvet, window-curtains and valances to match; mahogany washstand, ditto towel-horse; ditto wardrobe; ditto dressing-table and glass; three ditto chairs, original covering unknown, second covering, white dimity; large arm-chair, ditto ditto; Brussels carpet, hideous, with rug to match; bronze fender, steel fire-irons. Ornaments on chimney-piece: china shepherdesses and Paul Pry; a ditto sheep and dog, both couchant; a pair of very much soiled fire-screens. Above the chimney-piece, a portrait of Mrs. Isaac's mother, badly executed, and much cracked, in a frame that stood greatly in need of re-gilding.

In comparison with our humble belongings, this apartment was luxury itself; but in comparison with the splendour surrounding me in Miss Wifforde's dressing-room, Mrs.

Isaac's best bed-chamber hid its diminished head.

I was dreadfully frightened, as much, I may honestly say, by reason of the furniture as of Miss Wifforde, who began the conversation thus—

"I have some cause to believe that you are older in years than a stranger might imagine from your extremely childish appearance" (I winced at this remark), "and that you are, from the peculiar circumstances of your bringing up, older in mind even than in years."

Having arrived at which point, Miss Wifforde poured scent on her handkerchief, applied it to her brow, and commenced fanning herself, which were proceedings strange to my experience.

"For both of which reasons I have decided to talk to you about your future. Have you ever thought of it?"

The question was abrupt, and took me by surprise, "for both of which reasons," to quote Miss Wifforde, I answered vaguely—

"No, ma'am—that is, not much."

"Not much," she repeated, with that smile which only a woman in her rank knows how to smile.

Thinking of it all, I have a sort of momentary sympathy with those who rebel against centuries of cultivation.

"Not much—but how much?" I wonder why it is that the upper ten always unconsciously touch the French idiom when they are not dealing quite frankly with you, and know it.

Most of my readers have been, it may fairly be presumed, present at a cross-examination or subject to one. I felt just then as the poor wretch does who, after giving what he believes is truthful evidence, has to set his face to the opposing counsel, whose business it is to prove he has been telling lies. I was in for my cross-examination by a lady, and here it is:

"Not much, but how much?" was the question; and just as I might have answered Mr. Serjeant So-and-so, I replied desperately—

"While my grandmother was ill, I wondered what would become of me if she was never to get any better."

"I understand," said Miss Wifforde, "and then——"

"I beg your pardon, ma'am."

"What did you think after that?"

"I thought nothing, ma'am."

"And have thought nothing since?" This was interrogatory.

"My grandmother is well now, ma'am, and there is no need to think."

Since that hour I have heard of people getting checkmated unexpectedly, but I never saw such an evidence of it.

Miss Wifforde sat silent a few minutes, then she said—

"You are young and I am old, and the experience of the old is, that what has happened before may happen again; at any future time Mrs. Motfield may fall ill once more, and it is possible I—we—may not be at hand to help you."

I rose up; I was appalled. Here was death—a dual death—close at hand suggested in a single sentence.

"Oh, Miss Wifforde!" I cried, "do not talk like that, please don't!"

And I stretched out my hands to entreat her pity—all in vain.

"My child," she began—from that hour I always detested and distrusted people who called me, "my child" or "my dear," or indeed, to condense matter, "my anything"—"I trust your grandmother has many, many years of life before her. She has a wonderfully strong constitution, and her habits have been simple and regular, but still——" At this point Miss Wifforde abruptly broke off her sentence, and after a moment's pause began another.

"I told you I meant to talk to you about your future. There is no necessity for Mrs. Motfield's life or death to enter into the question. Sit down again, my dear. Our conversation has somehow drifted into an unpleasant subject, but we must try to forget that, and speak for the future of nothing excepting what is agreeable. I have been thinking much about you since that Sunday evening when we first met, and it seems to me a pity you should not receive such an education as might enable you to make your way in the world, no matter in what circumstances you may chance hereafter to be placed."

I grasped the sense of this remark, but not its drift, and so remained silent, although Miss Wifforde evidently expected some reply.

"As a rule," she recommenced, "I am not an advocate for highly cultivating the intellect of—" "the lower classes" I know now she meant in her heart, but she really said, "those who are not likely to have sufficient leisure in after life to enjoy the fruits of such early teaching; but there is no rule without an exception, and, as I said before, I think it is a pity you should not receive a thoroughly sound education. You would like to know as much as other girls of your age, I suppose?" she added, finding that unless she put a direct question it was vain to hope for any answer.

"Yes, ma'am."

"But there seems no chance of your ever learning much here."

I shook my head mournfully.

"Music now, for instance," she suggested. "You would like to become an accomplished pianist, to be taught singing——"

"It would vex grannie," I murmured.

"I think not," was the reply. "Indeed, I am sure not. Mrs. Motfield is much too sensible to allow prejudice to blind her in a matter where your interests are concerned; and if she saw that you could receive good instruction at a reasonable price, there can be no question but that she would only be too glad for you to be put in the way of taking advantage of it. Now near Fairport there are two ladies for whom I have the highest esteem, who take a limited number of pupils. Their establishment is less like a school than a home. You would have every opportunity there of obtaining a thoroughly sound education, and of acquiring such accomplishments as you may wish to gain. I have already mentioned the matter to Miss Brundall, and she is quite willing to receive you on equal terms with her other boarders, and at a cost which Mrs. Motfield can afford. Should you like that?"

"Like it! Oh, ma'am."

I could not say another word, my heart was too full for speech. Miss Brundall's was *the* school of Fairport—of the whole county, in fact. At it attended professors who had come all the way from London. A real French governess lived in the house; the young ladies sat in a great square pew at St. Stephen's Church. Miss Brundall's school was as much exalted above that at which my cousins were being educated as —as the great house was above our cottage. Miss Cleeves herself could not have desired greater advantages than were now offered to me. Like it! My face showed whether I did or not; and Miss Wifforde read its expression correctly.

"I am glad you are pleased," she said, evidently gratified at my delight; "I thought you would be. So the matter is settled. I shall ask Mrs. Motfield to let me provide your wardrobe."

I had forgotten Grannie—forgotten everything except the prospect of change, of beholding the sea once more, of being able to learn such things as Miss Cleeves had laughed at the idea of my not knowing. I had raised up a fairy palace for myself, and in a moment it was level with the earth.

"If you please, ma'am," I said, "I do not think my grandmother would like me to go to Miss Brundall's. I can't tell you how much obliged I am, but——"

"Stop a moment, child! What if the question be left for you to decide?"

"I do not know what you mean?" was my stupid reply.

"I mean this: I saw Mrs. Motfield this afternoon. I told her what I have told you. I pointed out to her other advantages likely to ensue from such a step, which you would be scarcely able to comprehend at present, and her reply was, 'I will leave it entirely to Annie. If you and she settle that she is to go, she shall go. It must be altogether as she chooses.' There is an unheard-of amount of confidence to place in a little woman no older than you are!" added Miss Wifforde, with a well-meant attempt at sprightliness. "So you see the decision rests with you, and none other."

I did not answer for a little while; then I said—

"Grannie would be so lonely without me."

"No doubt; but mothers are lonely when they send their children to school, and yet they send them nevertheless. Mrs. Motfield is quite satisfied that it would be a good thing in every way for you to accept Miss Brundall's offer. You are not strong. You have been mopish and dull lately, she tells me. You ought to be amongst other young people; you want change of air and scene and occupation. Besides, you have been in the habit of staying at Fairport, and Mrs. Motfield has gladly spared you to do so. You will be able to come home frequently, and tell all you have learnt and been busy about. I shall write to Miss Brundall to-night, and tell her it is settled."

What was I to say? what could I say? To me the prospect was alluring, and Miss Wifforde had evidently won my grandmother's consent.

I could only thank Miss Wifforde once again; I could only, the interview being virtually over, rise, and after going through that farce of hand-shaking, which it pleased the lady to perform, make my way out of the house, escorted to the hall-door by Hunter, who had been duly rung for in order to see me safely along the corridors and down that wonderful flight of stairs.

I should have shaken hands with her at parting had she permitted me to forget my new dignity so far. Instead of noticing my intention, she drew back; and making a little frigid and slightly satirical curtsey, she said, "Good afternoon, Miss Trenet," with an emphasis on the last two words which really made me feel ashamed of my name.

After all, it was not my fault that Miss Wifforde had taken notice of me; and greatly elated with my prospects, though with a certain consciousness that there was a drawback somewhere, I walked down the avenue and through the gates, and home along the sandy road, thinking as I went—thinking, I grieve to say, with an ever-increasing happiness—of how pleased I should be to go to school, and see Fairport once more.

As Miss Wifforde had truly said, I did want change of air and scene and occupation, and the very idea of change seemed to raise my spirits. Besides, socially I felt uplifted. My cousins could look down on me no longer, if I were once an inmate of Miss Brundall's school. No Motfield in his wildest dreams would ever have contemplated asking for the admission of a daughter into that select establishment. I should learn—Oh, what should I not learn! I should be able to play and sing; I would study hard and become a good French scholar; I would try to carry myself like Miss Cleeves; I would make grannie proud of me; I would bring back with me to the cottage news enough to fill it full from parlour to attic; I would send such long, long letters home! Castle after castle I built in the air as I sauntered along, enjoying as I had not done for months before the sights and sounds of nature.

Soft was the turf under my tread; green were the elm-trees in the Wifforde woods; calm was the distant landscape, lying still and quiet in the evening light. My heart was full of joy. It did not hold a care or a thought of care as I unlatched the little gate, and walked round to the back door, as was the custom when the front one did not stand ajar.

"I think the mistress is asleep," remarked our abigail, who met me on the threshold.

"I wont disturb her," was my answer;

and I entered the parlour so softly that she never woke.

She sat in her accustomed easy-chair, her head resting against the back, her face turned slightly towards the window. I wonder how it happened that the expression of it should have struck me then, as it had never struck me before! To the end of my life I shall not be able exactly to define what I thought and felt during that moment, while I stood looking at the worn sad face, at the lonely figure, at the thin hand which hung over one arm of the chair, at the grey hair smoothly braided under her widow's cap. I could see plainly that she had been crying. There were the traces of tears on her cheeks. There came even in her sleep now and then a little quiver of the eyelids and a tremor at the corners of her mouth that I could not bear to look at.

Where were my air-castles now? where the dream I had so lately pictured as a reality? By some sort of intuition I felt that if I went away I should break her heart; that she had left it to me to decide, because she would not in her utter unselfishness let her wishes or pleasures do violence to mine. In the expression of that changed face, which could not in slumber mask itself with a fictitious brightness, there was a meaning I was then too young to grasp. All I understood was, that I could not go away; that if I could help it she should never know I had wished even for a moment to go away.

I never gave myself a second for deliberation. More rapidly than I had built my house I razed it to the ground; out of the room I slipped as quietly as I had entered it.

"I am going out again for a few minutes, Mary," I said, as I passed through the kitchen; "I shall be back by the time grannie wakes;" and, that the click of the garden gate might not arouse her, I went along the paddock, jumped over the low hedge into the road, and then how I did run! I do not think a greyhound could have reached the gates of the Wifforde domain much quicker than I did that evening.

"You are out of breath, Miss," said the woman who had let me out so short a time before.

"Yes," I answered, "I have been runing. I want to see Miss Wifforde before —before they sit down to dinner."

"The first bell has not rung yet," she remarked.

"What is the first bell?" was my inquiry.

"It rings half an hour before the dinner-bell; you need not hurry up to the house, you have plenty of time."

And thus assured I slackened speed, even pausing now and then in order to recover my breath. There was no need for haste. I did not want to say anything then I should not be ready to repeat on the morrow. I had quite made up my mind. I was not afraid of speaking to Miss Wifforde now. I had settled upon the very words I should use. I hoped I should see her all alone in that same room where I had accepted her offer; but whether I saw her alone or not, or in the same room or not, I determined I would try not to be stupid, but tell her I could not go to Fairport, that I would give it all up.

As I was about to knock, Mr. Sylvester came and spoke to me. He was very kind; asked me how I was, and hoped Mrs. Motfield's health was perfectly re-established, and then inquired if I wished to see his aunt.

By this time he had turned the handle of the hall-door, and when I answered in the affirmative he ushered me into a small morning-room, where, after ringing the bell, he stood talking till a footman appeared, when he said—

"Inquire if Miss Wifforde can see Miss Trenet," and then continued talking, principally about his cousin.

How still the house seemed! What a contrast his quiet self-possession to the flurry and flutter of my own manner! How I envied Hunter her stately composure when she came to announce that Miss Wifforde would be pleased to see me in her dressing-room, and then preceded me in dignified silence along those passages which were becoming almost familiar!

That Hunter hated me I felt confident, though why she did so I could only vaguely imagine; and my courage was not increased by the wordless hostility of her manner.

She did not knock at her mistress's door on this occasion, but, opening it wide, announced "Miss Trenet," and then closed it behind me, not waiting to be told to go.

The half hour since I left Miss Wifforde had been sufficient to produce a metamorphosis in the apartment and in her. The blinds were pulled down and the curtains drawn across the windows. Wax-candles stood lighted on the chimney-piece and dressing-table, and were reflected from every mirror on the walls.

A jewel-case stood open, and I could see stones that almost dazzled me they were so bright, and gold bracelets, and chains, and rings. As for Miss Wifforde herself, she stood before the toilet-glass fastening a diamond brooch into a mass of soft net that covered her neck and shoulders, and she looked altogether so like my idea of a queen, that I remained with my lips parted when she turned towards me.

The sight is just as present to my eyes now as it was then. Trailing over the light carpet I see her ruby-coloured train trimmed with the richest lace; flashing amongst the velvet and lace that composed her head-dress was a spray of diamonds; her fingers, as she busied herself with the brooch, seemed to my imagination glittering with gems.

There was a dinner-party that evening at the Great House, though I did not then know it. Notables from ten and twelve miles distance were at that moment driving along various roads leading towards Lovedale. Decked out in lace and jewels that had been heirlooms for generations in the Wifforde family stood the eldest of "our ladies," ready to sweep down the staircase into the drawing-room and receive her guests; and there, in a dress which I had outgrown, in a second-best pelisse, in a last year's bonnet, stood I, Annie Trenet, beside a mirror that reflected back every detail of my shabby costume.

"I did not expect to see you again this evening," remarked Miss Wifforde, finding I remained as silent as though turned into stone.

Then, as if the sound of her voice had broken some spell, I began. How I ever uttered the words I came to speak I cannot tell, but they were spoken. It seemed to me that somebody else, not myself, was talking a long way off; the rush of the Love was in my ears, there came a mist before my eyes; and then in a moment it cleared away, and the rush of the waters ceased, and I heard my own tongue saying—

"I cannot go to Fairport; I cannot leave my grandmother."

"What folly is this, child?" and she put her hand open upon the table as she turned and looked angrily at me. "Have you gone crazy, or has Mrs. Motfield, to treat me with such an utter want of respect?"

"I cannot leave her," I repeated. "I will not. She was asleep when I got home, and if you had only seen how she looked, indeed, ma'am, you would forgive me."

"I do forgive you," she answered, putting her passion aside, and with an evident effort resuming her natural manner; "that is to say, I will forgive you on one condition—namely, that I hear no more of this nonsense. Now go," she added, "for our guests may arrive at any moment." And she was on her way to the bell-rope when I stopped her.

"Oh, Miss Wifforde, please, please do not be angry. You said it was to be left for me to decide, and I have decided. I cannot go; I could not leave her."

"Be kind enough to remove your hand from my dress," said Miss Wifforde. In my excitement I had seized her skirt, and when I released my hold, she shook the silk as though shaking off the taint of some loathsome reptile. "Now listen to me," she went on. "You must go to school, whether you please or whether you do not please, and I will tell you why. We cannot have Miss Cleeves back here until you are away. We are willing and wishful to advance your prospects in life, to give you the means of supporting yourself hereafter ; but we are determined that for the future our niece shall be debarred from an association which is as injurious to you as it is derogatory to her."

I stepped back as if she had struck me. She was so indignant at the bare idea of having her plans frustrated, that she never paused to weigh her words, or to consider how deeply they might cut. I had taken her by surprise, and in turn she had taken me.

After all, temper makes most people for the moment wonderfully alike. I could not have believed it possible for one of "our ladies" so nearly to resemble Mrs. Isaac Motfield as Miss Wifforde did in her manner at that moment.

"You understand me," she said, with a haughty gesture and disdainful turn of her head, that I had often noticed in Miss Cleeves, "distinctly ?"

"Yes," was my reply, "but I shall not leave my grandmother."

"Then you and your grandmother must leave Lovedale, and you can tell her I say so."

I waited for no more, but escaped from the room, tears of rage and mortification and terror blinding me. In my fright I ran up against Miss Hunter, whom I believe to have been listening outside; but without waiting to apologize, or even thinking of such a thing, I sped on, along the passage, down the staircase, across the hall, through the door, which happily stood wide open, and so out into the twilight. Through my tears I saw the lamps of many carriages, as they came slowly up the drive, but I never paused to look at the people those carriages contained. My own concerns were all-sufficient for me, and I was half way home before I remembered that I should frighten my grandmother to death if I appeared before her with red cheeks and eyes swollen by crying.

A little brook rippled across the common, and flowed beneath the road, and I knelt down on the grass beside it, and bathed my face with the cold water till I imagined it must look like my own again.

As I entered the kitchen, however, I was undeceived.

"Lord sake, Miss Annie, what have you been doing to yourself? You look as if you had seen a ghost. You are as white as a sheet, and all of a tremble."

"I am cold," was all the reply I vouchsafed, walking on towards the parlour, rubbing my cheeks the while, to put fresh colour into them.

My grandmother was awake.

"Where have you been, Annie, this long, long time?" she asked.

"At the Great House."

"But you came in from there an hour ago, Mary told me."

"I went back again; I had forgotten something."

She went on making the tea, and I stood beside the table, knowing I must sooner or later tell her what had passed, and yet not having the slightest idea how I should do it. After waiting for a little, she paved the way for me herself.

"Did you see Miss Wifforde, Annie?"

"Yes, I saw her," was my reply.

"And what did you and she settle?"—this slowly, and after a pause.

"*We* settled nothing," I answered. "Miss Wifforde said I should go to school, and I said I should not; that I could not and would not leave you."

She caught me to her heart with a great sob of relief.

"Oh, Nannie, I was so afraid!" she whispered; and then she loosened her clasp, and holding me from her at arm's length, asked what Miss Wifforde said then.

"Miss Wifforde said then," I repeated, "that you and I must leave Lovedale together, and that I could tell you so."

For a moment she seemed like one stunned; then she said—

"Well, if we must, we must; we shall go together, at any rate."

We did not talk much after that. We both sat silent for a long time, thinking each in her own fashion—my grandmother no doubt retracing the past, I busy with the present. Had I tried, I could not then have repeated Miss Wifforde's words; the very memory of them seemed to choke me.

I did not deserve them, I knew that. I had not asked Miss Cleeves to speak to me. I had never set myself up as a fit companion for her. I would have kept out of her way, if she would have kept out of mine. I had not been disrespectful to Miss Wifforde; I had a right to stay with my grandmother if I wished to stay with her, and she wished me to do so."

Vaguely I understood the unreasonable pride, the intense selfishness, the detestable despotism, that underlay Miss Wifforde's proposition. I was a something to be got out of the way, peaceably if possible; but when I would not go peaceably she showed that she meant to drive me off with contumely and reproach.

I sat in our little room, chafing in silence over the recollection of the cruel interview, wondering if the woman I had seen in so terrible a rage could really be the same who rebuked Miss Cleeves for her lack of courtesy.

I hated Miss Wifforde as much as I feared her. Mentally I called her every evil name my poor vocabulary of abuse contained; I ascribed to her every sin I knew of; I wished I had it in my power to do her harm; I thought I should like to hear of her being ill and in sorrow; but through all my tortuous meditations I kept one clear idea before me—I would not tell my grandmother what Miss Wifforde had said. For the first time I resolved to keep a secret from her.

At length we went to bed, both of us sad at heart, and yet both of us glad, because we had learnt how dear each was to the other.

All the night long I kept tossing from side to side—now dozing, now dreaming, now starting, never sleeping soundly—so that, when morning dawned, my head was aching so badly, that I could not lift it from the pillow; and I lay on hour after hour, waiting for that sleep which would, my grandmother declared, make me quite well.

At last it came. The cooing of the pigeons, the prating of the hens, the cawing of the crows, and the bleating of the lambs first mixed and mingled together, and then were heard no more.

How long that slumber lasted I cannot tell. I only know I awoke with a confused sense of some one standing by my bedside, and opening my eyes, I beheld Miss Wifforde!

"Lie still," she said, laying her hand on my shoulder as I was starting up. "I have come to beg your pardon. I was wrong yesterday evening. Will you forgive me?"

"Oh, Miss Wifforde!" I cried, "I will do anything you like, if you only let grannie stay here, and me with her."

END OF VOL. I.

www.ingramcontent.com/pod-product-compliance
Lightning Source LLC
Chambersburg PA
CBHW030810230426
43667CB00008B/1144